ADVANCE PRAISE FOR S(

C000041859

We live in a ministry culture where it can be confusing for churches to know how to gauge success. This book is a beneficial resource, rooted both in Scripture and our modern context. It clearly points us to our primary call to make disciples and practically describes how to be faithful to that mission.

—*Dr. Daniel Hyun,*
Church Partnership Team Leader
at Baptist Convention of Maryland/Delaware; Adjunct Faculty Member of
Church and Ministry Leadership at Lancaster Bible College

I had the privilege of teaching Kevin in multiple seminary classes and spending time with his family outside the classroom. Kevin consistently displayed not only a sharp intellect but a creative mindset. He has masterfully combined both those traits in this book. Biblically based, creatively written, and with a focus on application, I heartily endorse this work. It will force you, as it has forced me, to think about evangelism and discipleship in new and helpful ways.

—*Dr. Timothy Beougher,*
Associate Dean of the Billy Graham School of Missions,
Evangelism, and Ministry at The Southern Baptist Theological Seminary

Looking at Christianity in the United States, there is ample reason for discouragement. One noticeable concern is mission drift. Many congregations seem unclear about their mission in God's Kingdom plan. Further, they lack the ability to evaluate the fruitfulness of their present efforts and programming. Kevin Freeman, informed by Scripture and years of ministry experience, provides helpful analysis and encouragement from a foundational parable rooted in Matthew's and Luke's Gospels.

—*Dr. Kevin Smith,*
Pastor of Family Church Village in West Palm Beach, Florida

Kevin Freeman has given us a remarkably thought-provoking and practical book based on Jesus's two dynamic objectives in the Great Commission—to make and teach disciples. He helps us answer this important question: To what extent do we have these supracultural directives in balance? This is an immensely helpful book!

—Dr. Gene A. Getz,
Professor, Pastor, and Author; Founder of bibleprinciples.org;
Host of Renewal Radio

Evangelism and discipleship, as Kevin Freeman shows us, are not a bifurcated "either/or" but rather a "both/and" endeavor. Employing the Parable of the Sower and extrapolating it into future fictional generations, Freeman creatively shows how the church has abandoned Jesus's original plan of scattering the seed of God's Word in favor of ineffective and far less optimal alternatives. The resulting harvest has been mediocre rather than bountiful. But Freeman also shows a better way: one that appreciates the integral relationship between evangelism and discipleship to empower the church to make disciples who make disciples. As Freeman says, "The sustained success of both evangelism and discipleship is found when they operate in concert." This book will equip the church to do exactly that.

—Mark Dooley,
State Director of Evangelism at
Baptist Convention of Maryland/Delaware

Kevin Freeman lives his life with Great Commission intent. *Scatter the Seed* is a guidebook that not only outlines the importance of proper disciple-making—that special combination of evangelism and spiritual formation—but also presents a clear and reasonable look at how the true mission of the church can be restored. This book can motivate Christ followers toward fulfilling the Great Commission within their lifetime.

—Dr. John B. Brittain,
Associational Mission Strategist at
West Central Baptist Association, Missouri

One of the greatest callings for the American church today is to raise up disciples in the next generation successfully. There's a fine line between evangelism and effective discipleship; both must take place in their proper contexts to allow the Spirit to work. Anyone looking to be obedient in sharing their faith will benefit from this book. I'm grateful for Kevin, his heart for people, and his furthering of the gospel story.

—Ryan Shieh,
Author of Abiding: Living Life Abundantly;
Speaker; Divinity Student at Liberty University

Drawing on a well-known parable in this masterfully written book, Kevin Freeman examines the nature of discipleship, new methods of discipleship to be evaluated through the lens of Scripture, and the opportunities and challenges of following Jesus in our modern world.

As Kevin makes clear, discipleship is a simple concept. Jesus selected less-than-stellar men to be His disciples, then instructed them to make more disciples. Obedient discipleship is part of being a Christian. God's marvelous grace compels us to be disciples—to be made more like Christ wherever He has called us. It also compels us to advance God's mission of bringing salvation to the world.

After learning from this easy-to-read book, my fervent prayer is that, through God's Spirit, it will reignite our hearts to get back to the basics of evangelism and discipleship as Jesus instructed. It certainly has mine!

—Dr. Peter W. Teague,
President Emeritus of Capital Seminary
& Graduate School at Lancaster Bible College

This book is an absolute gem! Kevin's passion for the local church and its disciple-making efforts shines through. Thoughtful, practical, and truthful, he shines a light on an area in which far too many churches fall short: the making of disciples. I was encouraged, challenged, and convicted as I consumed this powerful work. Thanks, Kevin, for the reminder that we are called to make disciples, contributing to the next generation of people who will not only *say* "Jesus is Lord" but will *follow* Jesus as Lord!

—Tom Stolle,
Executive Director of the Baptist Convention of Maryland/Delaware

Scatter the Seed: Reviving Effective Disciple-Making in the Local Church is a must-read for any Christian wanting to refocus on fulfilling the Great Commission of Matthew 28:18–20. Kevin Freeman defines the nature of true discipleship and provides wise counsel to enable believers to be more effective in cultivating followers of Jesus. This book is engaging, practical, and firmly grounded in Scripture.

—Dr. Mark R. Meyer,
Director of Biblical Studies at Lancaster Bible College;
Pastor of Halethorpe Community Church

Kevin Freeman's approach to ministry is to integrate discipleship with evangelism, an often-overlooked strategy. He is like a modern-day Johnny Appleseed who believes that the Great Commission of Jesus Christ (Matt. 28:18–20)—going, baptizing, and teaching to obey—is indeed the church's mission and is best described through the organic metaphor of a farmer casting seed. The aim is to reorient Christians in their mission to make disciples and to depend upon God for growth and fruit. Freeman's ideas are based on sound research and years of experience in ministry—and are easy to understand. In a world of ministry fads that come and go, this book is a needed addition to help churches grow deeper in their understanding and practice of discipleship.

—Dr. Ron R. Blankenship,
Director of Missions for Montgomery Baptist Association
in Maryland; Adjunct Professor of Practical Ministry and
Biblical Studies at Washington University of Virginia

In a culture that offers many avenues for Christ followers to pursue, Kevin lays out a compelling message, explaining that at all times the Christian can and should embrace Jesus's Great Commission call to be the disciple He wants them to be. This book will help reinvigorate you and your leadership team toward God's call and realign it with a more effective and achievable ministry strategy.

—Maina Mwaura,
Minister, Public Speaker, and Journalist;
author of The Influential Mentor: How the Life and
Legacy of Howard Hendricks Equipped and
Inspired a Generation of Leaders

Kevin Freeman makes a compelling argument for balanced discipleship and evangelism in the church today. From the Parable of the Sower, Kevin helps us see the need to use time-honored methods for reaching and discipling people while being open to new methods in successive generations. The church has scattered the seeds of the gospel for over two thousand years, and in whatever time that remains, we must be adaptive and hardworking to reach and disciple more people. Kevin's book is an important work for the church and its leaders today. It's well worth your time and investment—read it with others to multiply its impact.

—Ken Braddy,
Director of Sunday School &
Network Partnerships at Lifeway Christian Resources

SCATTER

Reviving Effective Disciple-Making

THE

in the Local Church

SEED

KEVIN FREEMAN

Ballast Books, LLC
www.ballastbooks.com

Copyright © 2024 by Kevin Freeman

All rights reserved. No part of this book may be reproduced in any form or by any electronic or mechanical means, including information storage and retrieval systems, without permission in writing from the publisher, except by reviewers, who may quote brief passages in a review.

Scripture quotations are from The ESV® Bible (The Holy Bible, English Standard Version®), © 2001 by Crossway, a publishing ministry of Good News Publishers. Used by permission. All rights reserved.

ISBN: 978-1-962202-63-3

Printed in the United States of America

Published by Ballast Books
www.ballastbooks.com

For more information, bulk orders, appearances, or speaking requests, please email: info@ballastbooks.com

To Karen, for always nudging me toward distant goals to help them become reality.

TABLE OF CONTENTS

FOREWORD

*N*ot only is Kevin Freeman a skilled writer, but he is also someone who loves Jesus and has a heart for discipleship. *Scatter the Seed* is birthed out of Kevin's passion to challenge Christ followers to be the disciples that Christ has called them to be. In *Scatter the Seed*, Kevin connects my passion for evangelism to the importance of discipleship. The two, you will see, truly work only in partnership with one another.

If you have ever found yourself looking at church life and thinking that something just isn't quite working, this book may be exactly what you need. It will expand your horizons to reconsider what you may have taken for granted, and— without overwhelming you—it will help you and a leadership team chart a course toward alignment with God's plans.

My desire is that you, the reader, will get to know Kevin's heart for Jesus the way I have and dig into the words that God has given him to challenge us to live out the message of Christ more effectively.

I'm excited that Kevin has finally put pen to paper and laid out an exceptional body of work for the Body of Christ to live by and enjoy.

—Dr. Conway Edwards,
Pastor of One Community Church, Plano, TX

INTRODUCTION

*O*n April 14, 1935, an otherwise sunny Sunday after-noon turned to blackness for residents of the American Great Plains as billowing clouds of dust swept in on them. Sixty mile-per-hour winds blew clouds eastward all the way to the Atlantic Ocean. Black Sunday, as it became known, underscored the problem of the Dust Bowl. An increasing prevalence of dust storms wreaked havoc on the area, caus-ing many to flee their homes and their livelihoods.

The dust problem can be traced to poor farming practices. New mechanized equipment allowed for greater areas of planting, but there was little restoration to the soil. Grasslands were stripped for planting wheat or cotton, yet no cover crops were replanted. The exposed ground and lengthy drought led to erosion and dust storms. Many restorative farming tech-niques have since improved the land, but the lesson of the Dust Bowl still serves as a warning for farmers.

The church can heed the Dust Bowl's warning, too. Just as changed farming techniques promised better results but deliv-ered disaster, changed ministry tactics can leave a landscape of parched congregations longing for more visible spiritual fruit. When churches struggle to produce disciples, a parched culture can find itself inundated by a swirling storm of chaos.

One change in practices many churches have attempted is overspecialization in either evangelism or discipleship. While some areas of society enjoy seemingly infinite specialization, the church can go only so far. The Great Commission, given by Jesus before His ascension, commands His followers to "make disciples of all nations" (Matt. 28:19), a deliberate combination of evangelism and discipleship.

The mission of the church involves both, as well—the telling and the training. When churches overspecialize, evangelism becomes outreach that lacks the punch of what God had planned, and discipleship becomes education that may be informative but is not transformative. With a healthy balance of both, evangelism prevents the decay of discipleship, which in turn prevents the decay of evangelism. Disciple-making is the combination of these twin ministry endeavors.

This is the mission of the church. As you read this book, it is my prayer that you will recall this mission and see how it relates to your own church context. Sometimes the mission is obscured or even obstructed amid the hectic clutter of busy church calendars. When a church recalls its mission by combining evangelism and discipleship into disciple-making, it can begin to restore and redeem its ever-present programs and schedules. Part two of this book will help readers develop the church's mission and then recruit, evaluate, allocate, and motivate by that mission.

The Parable of the Sower is one of Jesus's most iconic stories to describe the hearts of those who hear the gospel. Throughout this book, the parable is continued and transported to future generations, as the farmers who follow Jesus (the Master Gardener) attempt to scatter seed and work the ground faithfully for the best possible harvest. Their changed methods and rediscovery of well-established farming techniques will help today's Christians remain faithful to the transformative impact of the gospel on their lives. Just as Adam was forced to work the cursed ground of a fallen world, Christians today find themselves spreading the gospel among people whose hearts are not aligned to the hope found in Christ. Recovering the mission—the Great Commission—will remind readers that following the principles of the Master Gardener will produce the best result in God's Kingdom.

So, who is this book for? Pastors, deacons, and other ministry leaders will find this book helpful to their own ministry contexts. Small group members may be encouraged to hold fast to the methods described in God's Word, as their faithfulness leaves space for God to do His work. Any Christian can benefit from this book, especially if it is read and discussed with others. It is my prayer that, by God's grace, the Lord would bear fruit in your life and ministry as you consider the principles discussed in the following pages.

PART ONE

Recovering the
Mission of the Church

CHAPTER 1

TIMES HAVE [NOT] CHANGED

New Farming Techniques

*O*nce there was a Master Gardener who taught his aspiring farmers about scattering seed. The story opens with an anecdote by the Master Gardener:

> *"A farmer went out to sow his seed. As he was scattering the seed, some fell along the path, and the birds came and ate it up. Some fell on rocky places, where it did not have much soil. It sprang up quickly because the soil was shallow. But when the sun came up, the plants were scorched, and they withered because they had no root. Other seed fell among thorns, which grew up and choked the plants. Still other seed fell on good soil, where it produced a crop—a hundred, sixty or thirty times what was sown. Whoever has ears, let them hear."*
>
> *The Master Gardener stayed with his farmers, training them to scatter seed and care for plants. Then he departed, leaving his farmers to carry on his work. The farmers scattered seed and saw crops multiply. This continued for generations. Some generations were more successful than others, but all of them knew that scattering seed was integral to growing crops. It was their job.*

Eventually, a new generation of farmers encountered a newfound difficulty with scattering seed. Perhaps it was harder than in previous generations, or maybe it just felt that way. For all their effort sowing, reaping was minimal. These farmers began to rethink the business of scattering seed. It seemed to them that the soil was resistant to their seed. Some areas had become hardpacked while other areas were so nutrient depleted that few arable plots existed. The farmers could almost sense hostility when they scattered seed, which made them feel uncomfortable. The seed scatterers began discussing their struggles as they considered how to respond.

"The seed is to blame," offered one farmer. "It may have worked well in the past, but it does not work well with today's constraints."

A few nodded in assent. They had, after all, used the same seed for generations. Could its germination rates have been reduced?

"I think the problem lies with the soil," countered another farmer. "Generations before us did not work the ground right, and we are suffering the consequences."

The notion that the farmers bore no responsibility for the current predicament found significant agreement. Whether the fault lay with seed or soil, the problem must have developed over time. The solution, they knew, was up to them. Was it time to change their methods?

With a decreased trust in the effectiveness of the seed, these soil-focused farmers shifted their focus to include working the soil more and scattering seed less. Improving the soil became their topic of discussion; after all, they were fully aware of the problem of erosion. In time, planting seed and growing plants became lesser priorities. Instead, they championed whatever cause focused on soil readiness.

Scattering seed diminished, and fewer plants grew. The soil-focused farmers blamed the lack of growth on the pH level, amount of clay in the ground, and moisture retention levels. They did not, however, associate these lower germination rates with a decrease in sowing seed.

A different discovery caught the eye of the seed-focused farmers: while their own crops failed to grow abundantly, weeds produced a bumper crop. These farmers shifted their focus to the weeds, looking for clues from the unintended crop—clues that might assist their own farming methods. Observation quickly turned to admiration.

"This weed sprouted here on its own," remarked an impressed farmer, "with no help at all."

"I think weed seeds are being scattered by the wind," explained another.

"And then the weeds grow up quickly and healthy," another farmer noticed. "Maybe they grow and spread better because they scatter seed on their own."

These farmers became convinced that scattering seed was less important than ever before. Perhaps learning to enjoy weeds would save them a great deal of heartache while keeping the soil intact.

Scattering had all but disappeared, and few crops grew. Weeds were plentiful, and so was the farmers' knowledge of the soil's needs. This kept the farmers busy, and they saw some measure of favor from advocates in the weed community. The farmers celebrated their fresh direction. No longer were they tethered to one specific type of seed; they had gained newfound support for their diversification.

Principle #1: Making disciples can happen only when people are changed by the truth found in God's Word.

You Were Farming So Well. Who Made You Stop?

In the Parable of the Sower, Jesus describes one activity for the farmer: scattering the seed. Hard ground, thorny weeds, and rocky soil exist, but the method of scattering seed was the same—and it has not changed in the past two thousand years. Crops still grow when seed is scattered. While on earth, Jesus spoke a great deal about the Kingdom of God, which He established while on earth and which will be fully realized upon His return. His Kingdom is His garden. Just as Adam and Eve had a garden to tend in Eden, the Lord calls the church to tend His Kingdom garden, to scatter the seed until His return. Making disciples of Jesus is the primary element of the church's mission.

While the church has changed since Jesus commissioned believers to make more believers, the call to scatter seed has not. Beginning around the middle of the twentieth century, some churches implemented changes that attempted to improve on Jesus's primary job description for the farmer. These modifications led to a decrease in evangelistic activity, the very seed-scattering process that draws a person to Christ. Even when outreach activities have flourished, many have strayed from evangelism and discipleship. In his letter to the Galatians, the Apostle Paul writes to a church that had abandoned the gospel for works-based practices. He writes, "You were running well. Who hindered you from obeying the truth?" (Gal. 5:7). A similar question may be posed to Christians today. What hindered the church from obeying its mission to be seed scatterers? Historical distinctions in the twentieth century reveal how the changes have occurred.

Struggle within the Church

The rise of liberal theology—beginning in Germany in the late nineteenth century and continuing in the United States—explains some of the consolidation of theology at the expense of evangelism. Conservative[1] Christians vigorously defended "the fundamentals" of the Christian faith, rightly perceiving the theological dangers of liberal drift. Where "fundamentalists" focused on sound theology, liberal thinkers focused on practical ministry. The danger of preferring the practical to the fundamentals may be best illustrated in the story of a train accident of an earlier era.

A train gate operator was on trial following a crash. His job was to wave a lighted lantern when an approaching train neared an ntersection at night. Oncoming wagons would know to stop, preventing collision. Under oath, the operator testified that he had been waving his lantern on the night of the collision, but the train collided with a wagon and subsequently derailed. Several died in the accident. The watchman and the railroad company were acquitted.

Following the trial, the railroad attorney congratulated the watchman for his testimony and the watchman replied,

"I sure am glad the other attorney didn't ask me if the lantern was lit!"

Theologically liberal churches that have strayed from the fundamental truths of God's Word are waving unlit lanterns. Those ineffectual lamps did not result in changed lives even though bellies were filled as surface-level needs were met. But the conservatives, eager to show their lighted lanterns were just that, were guilty of another sin: many failed to wave their lanterns for others to see. They remained hidden under an academic bushel, equally ineffectual for a world in darkness.

Growth outside the Church

When churches abandoned the job of seed scattering, parachurch ministries became popular, filling the void. Organizations such as Young Life began to proliferate on the American scene beginning in the 1940s, and the resulting changed lives poured in. During the same time, Billy Graham's astounding ministry took hold. Churches paid attention: they began to emulate the parachurch ministries. In the 1970s, church denominations began developing youth ministries, largely based on the model of successful parachurch organizations. Over subsequent decades, churches have followed these paradigms and attracted people to the extent that their approaches also become popular.

Are We Really Making Disciples?

The "attractional" church model attempts to draw people in through exciting methods with the goal that those people might come to faith in Christ. Many churches saw a surge of success with this method. Advertising works: if a church can successfully market to people who need a church home and demonstrate churches are not as strange as outsiders previously thought, then the church is on its way to numerical growth.

One of the most famous models of this approach was Willow Creek Community Church, which attracted thousands to its Chicago campus. It is hard to argue with success. But Willow Creek had the guts to argue with its own success. In 2007, they published findings known as the *Reveal Study*, which challenged assumptions that the church was developing fully devoted followers of Christ. Willow Creek had taken the attractional approach to its most successful conclusion—thousands of people fully assimilating into the church's programming. Yet amid the burgeoning worship attendance, small groups, and other initiatives, the church leaders found themselves second-guessing their own methods. They asked, "Does increased attendance in ministry programs automatically equate to spiritual growth? To be brutally honest: it does not."[2]

Despite other issues that plagued Willow Creek a decade later, one must applaud the leadership for their willingness to ask the hard question: Are we really making disciples?

The Core of the Mission

In His Parable of the Sower, Jesus instituted scattering seed as the primary job of a farmer. He described the same activity in different terms just before His ascension. In His Great Commission, the Lord gave one mandate: make disciples. Among all the myriad church ministries and activities, making disciples is the singular pursuit of the church. Yes, the church is composed of believers who gather as a church, observe baptism and communion, teach Sunday school, appoint church officers, and so on. But strip away all the other activities that happen at church, and you will discover that Jesus directed only disciple-making.

But most churches do not take such a minimalist approach. To be fair, Jesus described different activities that characterize making disciples—baptizing, teaching to obey, the "as you go" pursuit—but the calendar clutter typical to many churches diverts members from the centrality of disciple-making. Think of it this way: a church member might be able to pick disciple-making out of a lineup, but few would identify it as the primary purpose of the Christian.

The attractional church relies on a bifurcated disciple-making process. Outreach and evangelism have been separated for the purposes of drawing people to Christ, while discipleship has become the drip feed for the believers within the church's walls. Members attend a worship service each week, and many are involved in a Bible study, but *most* churchgoers are separated from labors to make new disciples. The result is a hard truth: many churches are subcontracting their evangelism efforts.

Believers often rely on church outreach programs to scatter seed. People are willing to hand out an invitation to the youth basketball league or children's day camp or a Super Bowl "Big Game" party. And a few prospects trickle in and come to Christ as result. But the energy it takes to make these events work is astonishing. In many cases, volunteer-led teams put together elaborate events, contributing countless work hours.

These outward-facing ministries bring with them a great deal of good. There is no reason to cancel your major outreach programs rashly, especially if some of them see meaningful results. One benefit that accrues: church members contribute time to pull off these events because they have discovered a way to use their talents and gifts to build God's Kingdom.

The concern: these activities are often carried out in a way that leaves guests with a murky understanding regarding the goal of the event itself. They lack a follow-up plan or a tie to the mission. The members who put on the event may not have been shown how their participation is connected to making disciples. Somehow, the outreach event has become an end in itself rather than a means of accomplishing the disciple-making mission. Too often, success is measured by how fun the atmosphere was or how people liked the silly hat the pastor wore.

Similar Outcomes

Churches who have embraced liberal theology are like farmers who have begun to distrust their seed. Salvation is no longer found through faith in Christ; it comes through justice-related causes instead. Supplying affordable housing, clean drinking water, addiction treatment programs, or basic foodstuffs are a poor substitute for the forgiveness of sins and an eternity spent with a loving God. Without faith in God, their endeavors—though laudable—are often skewed to helping humans flourish here on earth but not in eternity.

To add to the confusion, liberal churches must find new sources of authority as the natural consequence of rejecting the Bible's authority. They often look to new truth claims found in cultural causes. The breathtaking speed with which our society moves to new "truths" and causes puts the liberal church at a huge disadvantage, as their foundations must shift rapidly to maintain a solid structure. Worse still, a church that follows culture is never followed by culture. If people recognize that what exists inside the church can be obtained outside the church, they have no reason to attend; they can obtain what a liberal church offers through social clubs or charitable causes. Consequently, disciples are not made in these churches; absent eternal and transformational truth, their numbers diminish.

Before performing a fundamentalist endzone dance, churches embracing conservative theology must recognize they are not doing much better. Sure, they are faithful to affirm the gospel and they desire to make disciples, but many struggle to achieve the community impact they seek. Even within the church walls, leading people to vibrant spiritual growth is tedious. Attempting ever-new techniques of both outreach and discipleship often leaves churches increasingly distracted, disorganized, and dysfunctional. In their effort to find ministry success, church leadership may quickly adopt the latest fad that has sprung up among Christians. It may be a new study, movie, or outreach that promises to be the next magic bullet leading to transformation and revitalization.

This sort of well-intentioned disciple-making strategy often equates busyness with effectiveness. It involves throwing as many activities as possible against the wall and seeing what sticks. It, too, is a variety of the attractional model. Outreach programs may enjoy elevated levels of participation, indicating success, yet only a trickle of new members come from the effort. Discipleship programs may see a core of members in attendance with little growth. In well-established churches, there may even be a slight decline. The problem looms in everyone's peripheral vision; they sense it but cannot quite identify or address it. Because the outreach program appears to be doing well, they tell themselves that growth is just around the corner.

While theologically liberal churches do not seem to be making any true disciples, theologically conservative churches seem to make only a few despite all their jostling. Those who have the courage to ask the tough questions Willow Creek asked might come to the same gut-wrenching conclusion: our programs and energies to make disciples are not as effective as we want to believe.

Recalling the Mission

When Jesus commissioned the apostles to make disciples, He described the disciple-making process in three actions: going, baptizing, and teaching to obey. We will explore each of these so that we fully understand what Jesus meant, and we will look at supporting passages to help clarify the process.

Going

The first part of Jesus's command is to go. Some describe this in the participle form, meaning, "Make disciples as you are going." Others put the emphasis on "Go for the express purpose of making disciples." Many commentators believe it is a balance of both: we should make it a priority *to go*; we should make disciples *as we go*. How should we do that? Jesus illustrated how to make disciples as you go. Jesus was walking by the lake—He was going—and He saw two fishermen who were brothers casting a net into the sea. He called, "Follow me, and I will make you fishers of men" (Matt. 4:19). Sounds simple, right? When Jesus said, "Go and make disciples," He meant that we should go and make disciples. Many churches, however, have developed extensive programming to compensate for their struggle simply to go, ask people to follow Jesus, and help them grow in Him. Instead, they subcontract their outreach to programs where people *might* get a sense of the gospel if they stick around long enough.

Let me illustrate this from my own life. My neighbor is not a Christian. Because my church was starting some short-term, small group studies, I suggested he should host one in his home, invite his friends, and that I would lead it. My experience was not like Jesus's encounter by the Sea of Galilee: my neighbor did not exactly leave his net and follow Christ. Instead, he said he would have to run it by his fiancée. Later that day I told his fiancée about it in front of him, and she responded positively to the idea. Then my neighbor and I spent some time together, and he asked me more questions about my faith than I can count. The next day he told me he had already found one person to come to the study that he would host. Wow!

This particular event turned out to be like seed cast on stony ground, meaning the opportunity withered a bit, but the seed was cast. Could it be that we are not "going" enough to make disciples?

God continually scattered His people in the New Testament era. The church grew in Jerusalem, but people primarily stayed put, so God allowed persecution to scatter His people. God radically saved Saul (who became better known as Paul) and led him to become a missionary. Jesus made clear that the goal of the gospel is to take it "to the ends of the earth" (Acts 1:8).

Christians who *go* might go to a far-off land, but in the context of the local church, going is more often a state of mind. I might *go* to the grocery store, but do I *go*, eager to make disciples—or do I go simply to grab milk, eggs, a loaf of bread, ham, and a jar of queso? My grocery list should come second to my *go-share* list. When I go to the store with the goal of looking for opportunities to make disciples, I am going as Jesus described.

Baptizing

Jesus explained that making disciples involves "baptizing them in the name of the Father and of the Son and of the Holy Spirit" (Matt. 28:19). Any new disciple should be willing to identify publicly as a Christian and participate in Christ's death, burial, and resurrection through water baptism. There are denominational differences here, but the key is formal commitment to be a disciple.

Some churches seem to focus on removing barriers of commitment in hopes of reaching more people. If churches want more people to join, simply lower the threshold of commitment, right? While this may seem to make sense, lower standards often lead to unintended consequences. A diminished threshold results in diminished commitment. People rarely value what does not cost them. Baptism is a key commitment threshold in the life of a disciple that should not be removed.

Baptism expresses a believer's declaration of faith in Christ for salvation. This declaration takes place in a church where a believer comes under the authority of Christ and in covenant community with the local church. This is a huge step, and we dare not minimize it. In the discipleship process, a person has learned from other believers what it means to follow Christ, has demonstrated repentance, and confessed faith in Christ. Baptism becomes the public expression of the believer's commitment.

Teaching Them to Obey

Discipleship is not simply teaching Jesus's commands. It is teaching people *to follow* His commands. This is about more than semantics. The difference is one of knowledge versus obedience. Teaching for knowledge is about communicating

15

information. Teaching for obedience is about transformation. Informed disciples experience the comfort of learning without the discomfort of applying. Transformed disciples put their knowledge into action.

A trainer once ran an experiment with a group of Christian educators. Prior to the training session, he posted the text of Matthew 28:19–20 on a whiteboard. Verse 20 begins with the words, "teaching them to observe all that I have commanded you," but the trainer intentionally left out two words: "to observe." Later, the group read the verses and were asked if they spotted what was missing. Only a handful noticed the omission. This experiment may identify one of the challenges facing believers: many have a proclivity to learn the Bible without applying it. It is possible to study God's Word, to know it intimately, and never to observe it. Many universities have biblical studies departments headed by people who possess extensive academic knowledge of the Bible but who demonstrate little or no application of its truth. Christians believe that the Bible is living and active and is the source of personal transformation, but God wants His children to do more than believe in the theoretical power of His Word. He wants us to observe the truth in transforming our lives.

Is it any wonder that many churches emphasize information over transformation? How does this happen? The answer is likely found in any combination of the following possibilities.

Comfort. Teaching for information is easier than teaching for transformation. People tend to settle into what is most comfortable when there is no external prompting. Just as water seeks its own level, people tend toward a comfortable equilibrium that avoids the discomfort of application.

Poor Leadership. Church leaders must enforce expectations regarding what and how their teachers and group leaders teach. Sadly, this is rarely the case. Pastors often find themselves so busy with their own teaching and pastoral ministry that they do not know what is being taught to their discipleship groups by other teachers. Without oversight from leadership, teaching for transformation will diminish over time.

Low Expectations. People who grew up in classrooms at school may unsurprisingly expect their Bible study group to convey information without moving to application. Church leaders must provide training to their teachers in order to uphold the standards of the church. Even a good schoolteacher needs training to discuss spiritual truth. Churches must train teachers to be effective and provide ongoing training to that end.

Sin. Teaching for transformation puts us in enemy territory. Transformative teaching from the life-changing Word of God makes us a target of Satan. When people have unconfessed sin, and they refuse to repent, they become spiritually deadened and less likely to respond.

Unbelief. Even in churches where people hold the Word of God in high regard, unbelief may creep in. It often happens through syncretism, blending society's beliefs with Christian teaching, leading Christians away from truth. Although it may be well-meaning, syncretism can be more destructive than obvious heresy. People are sometimes blind to the diluting influence of mixing societal and Christian beliefs. It is no difficult stretch for unbelief to result when a person encounters clear teaching in Scripture but responds by saying, "Well, it cannot mean that, because we know . . ." Outside knowledge can sometimes inform our understanding of Scripture, but it can never replace biblical truth. From a transformation perspective, eroded trust in the Bible puts the learner in the driver's seat to pick and choose what to believe and what to ignore.

In the Parable of the Sower, recall the seed that fell among the thorns that grew up and choked the plant. Jesus said the thorns were worldly desires, and much of our Christianity looks like that. Christians may maintain a few beliefs that do not align with Scripture, but what is the big deal as long as it is just a few weeds? The truth is, weeds usually outgrow the plant, absorb the sunshine, steal the water, and stifle Christian growth.

The prophet Jeremiah came at this truth with a different metaphor: God's people had rebelled from the spring of living water, having dug their own cisterns to store water, but these self-dug, cracked vessels could not do the job. The point was clear: spring water is better than cistern water. Cool, refreshing, and vibrant beats stale, stagnant, and seeping every time. Teaching to obey commands is challenging, yet vibrant and refreshing. Teaching to know commands but failing to act on them is demotivating and vapid.

Reengaging the Mission

How well is your church carrying out the mission given by Christ? Which activities are distracting from that mission, and how can you discover them? The next chapter will address programs that obscure and obstruct the church's disciple-making mission and provide a framework toward focusing programs on Kingdom growth. Later chapters will help your church develop a more localized mission understanding to help align your ministries around it. Such alignment will provide fertile ground for leadership development, energize your people, and point them toward what matters most: making disciples who make disciples.

Questions to Consider

1. Why is it important for a church to proclaim salvation through faith in Jesus Christ alone?

2. How strong is your church's confidence that spiritual growth happens as Christians learn to obey God's Word?

3. Which efforts in your church are most effective at making new disciples of Jesus?

4. What factors distract your church from its mission to make disciples?

5. How are you personally contributing toward disciple-making efforts in your church? How about in your daily life?

CHAPTER 2

ASSESS THE CLUTTER

Ant Farmers

The farmers who discounted the power of the ancient seed stopped sowing and eventually went out of business. After all, their only harvest was weeds. The other soil-focused farmers observed this failure and knew the importance of growing crops, but they still questioned whether simply scattering seed was enough. They focused on the hard soil instead of sowing seed. This group concluded it would be more comfortable for everyone involved if they no longer scattered the seed but simply offered the seed to soil that was interested. To them, there is nothing worse than offending soil by scattering seed upon it. Better to secure consent before scattering.

"But how will the soil know we have seed?" one farmer asked.

The perplexed farmers deliberated on this quandary. On one hand, soil seldom inquired about seed. On the other hand, farmers who cared about the soil knew the soil would be better off if plants were growing in it. This prompted them to develop new techniques to appeal to the soil, perhaps even softening it up so that the soil was well tilled and fertilized to make it ready to receive the seed.

"We can use newsprint to cover soil and keep it moist and shaded," suggested one wizened, old farmer. "It will keep out the weeds and make the soil happy."

The farmers loved this idea! As they excitedly discussed it, they decided that the newsprint should include information about their seed. That way, the soil would learn about the available seed when it sought out more newsprint. Ream upon ream of newsprint went out with friendly information about seed.

Left unasked were questions that lingered in the back of many farmers' minds. Why would soil without plants want to come to us for newsprint? Or what about soil that already has weeds? Even so, though it took several reams of newsprint, a few patches of soil did develop interest in seed—and the farmers celebrated their success.

But this presented an unanticipated problem: much of the soil still lacked seed. So, the farmers again convened to develop new ways to cultivate the soil. What could possibly generate the soil's interest in seed? They continued to puzzle over this until one farmer's eyes lit up. "What if we hold events that the soil would enjoy?"

The more they discussed this idea, the more excited they became, but what would appeal to the soil?

"Ants!" cried another farmer.

Immediately, the farmers began developing ant-related events that the soil would love. The idea was simple:

invite soil to events that involved ants. It all made sense. Ants cultivate the soil. They make it feel useful. The soil would enjoy the ants, trust the farmers, and learn about the seed that was available to them. No soil would be offended in the hosting of ant-related events.

Oh, what events these farmers created! And oh, how the soil loved the ants!

The ants tunneled in the soil, loosening it to allow the rain to soak in. The soil enjoyed the varieties of ants the farmers introduced to them. Some were athletic, giving the soil a taste of exciting recreation. Other ants were musical, entertaining the soil. Some were older, bringing wisdom to the soil. Others were young, offering energy. A couple times a year, the farmers even offered candy-coated ants, which was a real hit!

The farmers enjoyed how busy they were. Events with ants took a lot of time, money, and energy. It was grati-fying to see the success of these events. Before long, the farmers began to recruit new farmers whose sole job was to manage ants and their events. These were called ant farmers.

Ant farmers had a demanding job. The ant events took so much time and energy that the ant farmers did not have much time to scatter seed. Not scattering seed, however, was not a problem. Crop farmers could always scatter seed on the soil, leaving ant farmers time and resources to please the soil with ants.

The soil enjoyed the varieties of events, and the events saw a variety of soils co-mingling. The farmers noticed that much of the soil already had plants growing in it;

there was no need to scatter seed on it. Some of the soils came from neighboring farms. The farmers had some initial misgivings about this development—attracting soil with germinated seed scattered by other farmers was not their goal—but their apprehension quickly disappeared when they realized that sometimes those soils decided to stay on their farm. In time, the farmers understood their role included providing ant events for all soils, even those from neighboring farms.

Another benefit to the new farming strategy came when the ants sometimes carried seed that germinated and grew. This elated the farmers! If they held more ant events each year, they could count on new plants growing in their soil, and although the events took much of their time and energy, they were busy in the business of farming.

One farmer proclaimed, "If even one plant grows from our one thousand farmer hours, it is all worth it!"

The other farmers gave hearty assent—although no one asked if that one plant would have grown in the soil without their ant efforts. Considerations like that were often avoided. No one thought to ask a related question: if those same one-thousand farmer hours had been directed differently, would the harvest have been greater?

On many farms, the number of plants being harvested was shrinking, but the number of soil enriching events was growing. Some farmers found it easier to focus on the events than the plants themselves.

"Surely the Master Gardener would approve," many farmers concluded. The farmers became so consumed

with ant events that many of them grew less familiar with the art of scattering seed. Years passed, and many farmers became soil experts who knew nothing about how to sow seed.

Principle #2: Effective church programs create clear disciple-making pathways.

A Clear Mission

The hope of the gospel is found in the clear mission of Christ: to save His wandering sheep. The prophet Isaiah declared, "All we like sheep have gone astray; we have turned—every one—to his own way; and the LORD has laid on him the iniquity of us all" (Isa. 53:6). The effect of sin on this fallen world means people are prone to stray. For the one who has not come to faith in Christ, straying from the truth has already occurred. Believers, redeemed by the blood of Jesus, can keep from straying through the power of the Holy Spirit in them, but we remain susceptible to wandering from the things of God.

We can all identify with the first stanza of "Come Thou Fount of Every Blessing," in which Robert Robinson wrote of his pre-conversion years, "Jesus sought me when a stranger, wand'ring from the face of God." Yet now as a believer, he admits the problem of drifting away remains: "Prone to wander, Lord, I feel it; prone to leave the God I love." This wandering, this drifting, does not exist merely at the personal level. When individual Christians who are each prone to wander join a local church, that local church will be prone to wander too. It is no wonder then that churches are disposed to experience mission drift, the tendency to stray from the mission given them by Christ. Discipleship is the antidote to mission drift, both personally and collectively. This is what the Apostle Paul wrote to Titus: "For the grace of God has appeared, bringing salvation for all people, training us to renounce ungodliness and worldly passions, and to live self-controlled, upright, and godly lives in the present age" (Titus 2:11–12).

Making disciples is the mission, the essence of what Christians are called to do. It is what God calls faithful churches to do. Sometimes, however, churches invest in all kinds of activities instead of making disciples. Think about how time is spent in some of the following areas of your church. Consider the time and resources consumed inside of well-meaning activities that fall into the category of "prone to wander," or mission drift: Sunday school, recreation programs, prison outreach, Vacation Bible School (VBS), choir and worship teams, ladies Bible studies, men's breakfasts, the senior adults Christmas party, monthly food pantry, the knitting ministry, and so on. None of these is deficient in and of itself, but in a church of people who are prone to wander, not all of these contribute directly to Christ's disciple-making mission.

Remember, for a church to remain true to its calling, all its activities could cease, so long as it is making disciples. Programs are a primary, corporate means to make disciples, but without intent, these programs often lose definition over time. Although programs are meant to achieve this disciple-making mission, many churches have incrementally added them such that, over time, they have grown to obscure or obstruct the church's mission unintentionally.

Obscuring the Mission

Every time a church approves a new program, it affirms that the activity lies within the scope of what Jesus called a church to do. For example, worship services affirm that the church should gather to give praise to God and sit under the preaching of her pastor. Sunday school or small group ministries affirm the understanding that believers should join in interactive Bible study to wrestle with truths and better conform to the image of Christ. Those examples are the easy ones, tied directly to disciple-making endeavors. What is more difficult to discern are other ministry ideas that have no defined aim toward making disciples. Good ministries do not become great ministries for want of strategy.

VBS is a good example. Consider a church where VBS has been a staple outreach program for decades. A sizeable number of children who attend already know the songs and can teach the motions to the music leader. Why? Because this is their third VBS this summer! They and their parents belong to a church down the road, and VBS at a neighboring church becomes an opportunity for the parents to have some kid-free time or another date night. In other words, VBS degrades to good, clean fun, but it is not intentional discipling of the next generation.

There is nothing wrong with a church reaching out to these families in a Kingdom-minded way. Even from an outreach perspective, a church might determine VBS is the best way to reach the ten percent of attendees who have no church. They are happy to serve all the children but focus on relationships with the unchurched. In many churches, however, crucial strategic discussions do not happen; the right questions are not being asked. If they were, VBS leadership might take measures to increase participation from unchurched families. Some churches, for example, limit registrations to those with invites from church members until a specified open-registration date. Others create opportunities for additional connections with families who have no church. By leveraging opportunities to make disciples, VBS can become more mission aligned.

Unclear Strategy

Taking the time to strategize about a ministry can move it toward mission alignment. A mission-aligned ministry can be defined as one that follows a plan that contributes to disciple-making in the local church. Too many church leaders are not used to strategizing like this. To add to the struggle, most churches have well-established ministries with solidly entrenched understandings of what a ministry does. The church can become filled with existing ministries that, though positive, are not mission-aligned. Churches fail to have a direct strategy or evaluative tool for how this or that activity contributes to the church's call to make disciples.

The problem is not that our ministries are antithetical to the church's call: the problem is that they are off by a few degrees. Aircraft navigators know that when plotting a course, being off by even one degree could put them several miles away from their desired destination. As the church moves forward, what at first seemed to align with its call drifts away from the central, disciple-making goal of the church. Multiply that trend by several ministries with numerous intentions, and you end up with a church that expends a lot of ministry energy with little strategic thinking and minimal results. The church activities sprawl, rendering it stretched and busy, but lacking considered, mission-driven thought. A church that does not enforce its call to make disciples may end up with several well-intentioned but vestigial ministry appendages that do not contribute to its mission. This is not a good look for the bride of Christ.

Confused Mission

The greater the scope of activities, the greater the possibility for confusion regarding the church's call. Programs can obscure this call if they are not intentionally tied to the pursuit of making disciples. Once again, there may be good initiatives, but they lack mission focus. Obscuring the church's call can normalize ineffective strategies for everyone involved. On the one hand, those served by the ministry are not successfully drawn in to become disciples and grow deeper, while on the other, those serving begin to confuse what they are doing with what God called the church to do. Many involved church members may be unable to state clearly how their efforts contribute to making disciples. The less obvious the connection a program has with making disciples, the more clearly such a connection must be developed and explained by church leaders. Without this, church members may fail to view church ministry in terms of God's top priority to make disciples.

For simplicity's sake, consider a church that has only one program apart from worship: small group Bible study. Everyone is encouraged to join a small group. There is little confusion about the message; the church believes people should grow in Bible study together as a key element in making disciples. In time, this church introduces a second activity: a weekly board-game night. Now the bulletin publicizes two weekly events, and pulpit announcements include "come one, come all" invitations to both. Some will attend small groups, others will attend game night, and still others will attend both. What worshippers implicitly hear is that there are two church-endorsed activities for them to attend. While some know that Bible study is imperative, others may see both events on equal footing—after all, Christians should fellowship and have fun together. If not communicated clearly, the multiple offerings may allow programs that are not part of a disciple-making strategy to confuse people about the real mission of the church.

Pastors and ministry leaders must champion the call to state how each program contributes to disciple-making, and then evaluate the effectiveness of each. Anything less may result in members who do not understand the necessary dependency. The more the church's call is obscured, the more that call will be ignored.

One of my favorite TV shows when I was a teen was *Malcolm in the Middle*. This sitcom featured teenage boy-genius Malcom, whose family of six was the trashiest, most dysfunctional family on the block. In one episode, parents Hal and Lois clean out a closet that had been junked up for years. Their all-day project created interesting clutter that filled the rest of the house. At the climax of the episode, Hal and Lois discovered a working toilet tucked in the back of what they thought was a closet. With joy on their faces akin to a couple learning they are going to have a baby, Hal and Lois embrace and proclaim, "We have a second bathroom!" The closet was not a closet at all! It was a forgotten bathroom. In an ironic plot twist, they kept their discovery a secret, filling the space with boxes again. In time, even Hal and Lois forgot the bathroom existed.

Church programs can become like those boxes: they obscure the purpose of the church. A church with cluttered programs will yield a similarly cluttered understanding among members regarding its mission. Clarity comes when all programs can positively answer the question, "How will this program be designed to help us accomplish our mission to make disciples?"

Obstructing the Mission

Bevies of uncoordinated programs do more than obscure the mission. They obstruct it. Have you ever attacked the trivial items on your to-do list first? You expend most of your energy on the petty things, leaving less time for the more important things. It usually ends up leaving you frustrated. Churches fall victim to this error all the time.

Understand the Energy Quotient

Every church has an energy quotient. Church members have a finite amount of time to accomplish ministry programs. Divide the available time by the ministry needs, and you have your quotient. This is more conceptual than quantifiable, but it helps clarify the problem facing many churches: an abundance of programs keeps people preoccupied such that more important ministry objectives are not met. Many people do not volunteer because they are too busy.[3]

Or in many cases, this may reflect a lack of interest. People often volunteer fewer hours because they do not perceive the value in the activity. If you want strong volunteers, provide them with a compelling reason to serve. Volunteering increases when people understand the value of the cause. Churches with programs that tie in with their mission will have a high energy quotient.

A church without a clearly stated, disciple-making mission may end up with programs that fritter away the energies of its members. A church basketball night is a classic example. If ten members are involved in a weekly adult basketball program, but there is no direction given to help that program contribute to making disciples, ten members are in a program that obstructs the church's mission. Could the church see fruit from this program as basketball players become Christians and join the church? Yes, but that fruit will be minimal without a clear strategy. When programs are not focused on the mission of the church, members can become confused. They are encumbered with activity that does not help make disciples.

Churches often find themselves in this situation. For instance, a particular effort may do an excellent job reaching those apart from the church, but it does not have a clear path to help them develop faith or any eternal connection to the Lord. That is, while they may come to the church property, few come to a church service. The ones serving know they have a program with exciting potential, but they have not been trained to funnel people toward developing faith. This can lead to frustration when appeals are made to get involved: hearers may ask, to what end? Over time, people become disillusioned for lack of a strategy. In turn, serving members, whose numbers are few, may become overwhelming. A lot of seemingly great ministry activity will not yield more disciples if those who attend are there only for the program as an end in itself.

Eventually, programs like this fold and leave disappointment behind them. Busy members who wanted to be effective for Christ became discouraged. Those who stopped serving in that program did so because they could not see a clear connection between the program and making disciples. The church's energy quotient decreases as some were tied up in a great ministry idea that was not fully connected to the mission. In the end, willing workers may be less willing to jump at the next ministry opportunity.

Divided Ministry Interests

When a woman poured expensive perfume on Jesus's feet in an act of devotion, Judas objected—but not out of altruism. He complained that the perfume could have been sold and the proceeds given to the poor. In reply, Jesus made a startling assertion: "You always have the poor with you" (Mark 14:7). In other words, "It is better to invest in My feet than in poor people." It is better to pour out treasures in devotion to our Savior than simply to spread resources around that do not connect people to Christ. Jesus-focused ministries will cut against the grain of many of our Christian sensibilities.

Helping the poor is good, and so are other programs in the church, but the less these are focused on the person of Christ, the more they detract from the mission He gave us. Poor people need a leg up, but they need Jesus more. Athletes could use an outlet for basketball, but their real need is Jesus. If we want to help people, most of our energy must be devoted to honoring Christ. A church with divided ministry interests cannot reflect its singular devotion to Christ.

Now, before canceling your basketball or soup kitchen ministry, ask some questions. How can those to whom we minister be blessed by our remarkable dedication to Christ through this ministry? As volunteers expend energy in this program, how can their energy help make disciples? What pathways can we develop to build the church—not the entire membership, but those who are thriving learners—through our efforts? If you cannot develop a way to get there, do not continue or initiate that ministry. Do not suck people's energy away from the mission.

Program Killer

Jesus was not afraid to evaluate and discontinue some of His ministry programs. One of His most famous miracles occurred when He fed the five thousand. The miracle was so popular that people got into boats and crossed the Sea of Galilee to follow Him. Others hiked its perimeter to see Him again. When they found Him, Jesus announced He was discontinuing His feeding ministry. He told them, "You are seeking me, not because you saw signs, but because you ate your fill of the loaves. Do not work for the food that perishes, but for the food that endures to eternal life, which the Son of Man will give to you. For on him God the Father has set his seal" (John 6:26–27). In other words, Jesus declared the ministry was failing to make true followers of Him, so He put it on pause. There was no clear pathway from the "fish and loaves" outreach ministry to the Bible study groups. During this conversation, Jesus explained the point of the miracle was for people to see Him as the Bread of Life, because that pathway in fact led to Him. The result was a lot of grumbling from the people, who were more interested in the food than the Savior.

If Jesus evaluated and changed a ministry that was not having the intended results, should we not do the same? Christ's "feeding program" was of course different from modern-day food ministries, but His willingness to adjust tactics is a model for us to follow. His energies were creating numerical growth but not spiritual growth. How often do we measure the numerical growth of our ministries without measuring the spiritual steps people take as a result? How willing are we to change or even stop a numerically successful ministry that is not producing disciples? The answer will identify your priorities.

Programmatic Energy Knots

Have you ever had your muscles tense up into "knots"? A massage can relax them, allowing the muscles to return to normal function. When a knot develops, the muscle is expending energy by tensing up. It is more than just uncomfortable; it is extracting energy and making you more tired. Knots do not contribute to the healthy function of the muscle or the body. They always detract.

Many churches oversee programming that creates knots in their ministry muscle. These knots, which ironically often form when we are trying to build muscle, can instead tie it up and undermine what God called the church to do. The good news is that ministry knots can be massaged so that they begin to support the mission. This requires honest evaluation—a difficult step with beloved programs. People may defend a ministry knot, claiming "no pain, no gain" when, in fact, the pain is the result of a workout that has yielded dubious results. It is a knot.

Disciple-Making by Osmosis

Churches often justify their engagement in multiple ministry efforts that have no clear path toward making disciples by arguing that the sum of their efforts results in the making of disciples. We could call this making disciples by osmosis. According to this concept, churches develop all sorts of outreach programs to attract a variety of people to their campus. The intended result is that people will become familiar with and join the church. Exposure to the church will help people see the goodness of the church so that they will take steps to join. Most often, this approach falls short. It's not safe, and it doesn't work. Let me show you what I mean.

Recently, people in my part of the country joined together to ban giving money to panhandlers. The slogan that the county created was, "It's not safe. It doesn't work." The argument: although kind people were attempting to help the panhandlers, their acts of goodwill were not helpful. Traffic-related accidents made panhandling a safety issue, and in the long-term, the giving did not actually help the panhandlers. Hence the slogan. A similar slogan could be applied to the discipleship-by-osmosis approach: "It's not coherent. It doesn't work."

Osmosis discipleship lacks coherence. People may believe program attendees will become disciples simply by being on the church campus. Any one program is one link in a long chain that guests follow on their way toward Christlikeness. But in many churches, there is no chain: there is merely a collection of disconnected links. If outreach efforts are not tied to a coherent strategy, spiritual growth will be minimal—or missing altogether.

Sometimes, our omnipotent, sovereign, and gracious God will produce fruit even through our less-than-strategic ministry efforts. By His grace, we will see changed lives. But that same God has called churches to organize our efforts effectively, entrusting the task of making disciples to us. This means churches have a responsibility to connect ministry links in a chain that strategically develops Christlikeness.

Developing a Disciple-Making Strategy

Each church is responsible to understand its mission to make disciples, followed by developing a strategy to pull it off. If there is no growth, check to see if you are scattering seed. Jesus embodied seed sowing as the strategy for making disciples. His method is much simpler and far more effective than our ideas. This does not mean that our means are wrong, but we nonetheless seem to employ means that fail to make disciples. In the chapters ahead, you will find a plan for your team to discover the mission of the church, to develop a strategy to make disciples, and then to orient ministry practices around that strategy. But before moving forward, we must explore common misconceptions regarding evangelism and discipleship. It is these misconceptions that keep many churches from flourishing.

Questions to Consider

1. Which programs in your church require the most energy from people?

2. How effectively can people connect their involvement in these programs to disciple-making?

3. What program "energy knots" have developed in your church? How can these programs make better connections to making disciples?

4. In what ways has a "discipleship-by-osmosis" approach perhaps taken hold in your church? How can you incorporate a more direct disciple-making approach?

5. What percentage of participants in your church's outward-focused ministries are unchurched people?

CHAPTER 3

THE SEPARATION PRINCIPLE

Plant Health Awareness

The surge of ant farming practices can be explained, in part, by the simultaneous interest in increased plant health. Like ant farmers, other farmers became specialized, giving rise to plant-health farmers. Growing existing plants was something they knew the Master Gardener cared about, so they began to give those plants individualized attention. Instead of scattering seed on bare soil, they spread nutrients on growing plants. The plants loved these nutrients and the farmer's undivided attention!

As the plant-health farmers studied their craft, they made important discoveries. First, potted plants looked healthier than field plants. This may be because managing plants works best when one can control individual growth. The farmers purchased many pots in which to place these growing plants. Several varieties of pots were produced to accommodate the varied sizes and root systems of the plants. The plant-health farmers led periodic repotting campaigns and launched studies like "How to tell when you are root-bound" to guide the plants to consider their own personal health. Never had plants been afforded such a high degree of introspection. And introspect they did. Using tools provided by the farmers, these plants were able to discover their stamen type and how this knowledge could make them happier plants. They made use of objective measurements on their pollen counts. They especially liked how the farmers arranged them when their flowers were in bloom for the most creative and colorful display. This practice itself became another soil event that mostly attracted plants from other farms, and farms often competed for the best displays, with the successful ones luring a few potted plants to their own farms.

The plant-health farmers made a second discovery. They learned that greenhouses provided a more consistent growing environment. Drought led to withered plants, and excessive rain was even worse. While farmers at some farms worked the land to develop irrigation and drainage techniques, most opted for a different solution. Plants had for too long been subjected to harsh winters and dry summers. Climate-controlled greenhouses would eliminate all difficulties from the outside world. Because many farms had already potted their plants, this was an easy adjustment. The plants thrived in the optimal warmth and humidity of their perfectly managed environment. Their roots did not have to seek the water, for water always came in just the right amount.

The farmers eventually noticed that potted plants in greenhouses had difficulty reproducing. In the old days, seeds from the plants used to be collected after a growing season. Now, however, the plants were pruned for *their blooms, which were often picked off before the fruiting stage. Any fruit produced was used to fertilize and nourish those same plants, again with stellar results. The farmers, not wanting to deprive their plants of these natural nutrients, did the next best thing: they ordered seed from a catalog. This, they argued, was in fact better than the old method, because the companies that produced such seed were able to breed out unattractive peculiarities often found at local farms. The soil attracted to ant events had developed an expectation for specific varieties of seed anyway, so this better served their needs. There was also an increased demand for a broader variety of plants, which the catalog could easily accommodate. Each pot of soil could be given a seed packet of its own choosing.*

Interestingly, the rise of ant events coincided with the rise of greenhouses. The plants were more reliant than ever on the farmers to do the farming, but the edifices in which they were housed—and potted—left little with which to argue. Clearly, these endeavors were successful. Some farmers noted with apprehension that their plants now had little to do with reproduction; they also found that for the first time in farming history, the soil now had a voice in deciding what seeds were planted in it. Although this seemed unnatural, the farmers had little time to ponder this dilemma. They were too busy catering to the needs of plants and soil alike.

Principle #3: Sustained dynamic ministry must combine discipleship with evangelism; this is the essence of a church's mission to make disciples.

What God Has Joined . . .

In Mark 10, Jesus addresses the subject of divorce and stresses God's will for a husband and wife to remain in the marriage covenant for life. Jesus makes it clear in this statement: "What therefore God has joined together, let not man separate" (Mark 10:9). These powerful words describing the union of husband and wife can be invoked for evangelism and discipleship—the two tasks God has commissioned us to carry out. Unfortunately, many churches have inadvertently divorced evangelism from discipleship in a misguided effort to increase their effectiveness through specialization. Apart, however, evangelism and discipleship soon grow unstable.

In the 1950s, James Watson and Francis Crick, building on the scientific discoveries of others, discovered the physical structure of DNA—a discovery that has led to massive innovations over the decades. One of the perplexing facets of human DNA is how the complexity of creatures reduces to four chemical components: adenine, thymine, guanine, and cytosine. Their research revealed a unique structure on which those chemical components formed base pairs. It turns out these base pairs are singly enabled by the iconic double helix—no other configuration could work. Just as the building blocks of life cannot be arranged without the supporting structure of the double helix, so the life and growth of the church require the twin strands of evangelism and discipleship in concert. Evangelism and discipleship comprise the DNA structure of the Great Commission.

Jesus looked at this disciple-making DNA structure as one unit, but many churches have divided it into evangelism *and* discipleship, creating a bifurcated approach. Only by viewing these two strands in parallel can a church conduct its mission. In other words, a church must operate within her DNA design. To understand the effects of this design, it is helpful to define the terms surrounding it.

Defining the Terms

Evangelism is sharing the good news of Jesus Christ so that others will respond by placing their faith in Him for salvation from their sins. The Apostle Paul writes in Romans, "How beautiful are the feet of those who preach the good news!" (Rom. 10:15b). The person who comes to faith in Christ not only grows in Him but shares about His love. Part of the Christian's job is to tell others how they can become Christians. The Bible puts it this way: "Therefore, we are ambassadors for Christ, God making his appeal through us. We implore you on behalf of Christ, be reconciled to God" (2 Cor. 5:20). So, the person whose life has been forever altered by the grace received through faith in Christ is on a mission to proclaim that same message to others.

Discipleship, put simply, is becoming like Jesus by following Him. This is an intentional process, an act of the will that requires leaving one's own path to walk with Jesus. Notice that when our Lord called Levi, the tax collector abandoned his tax booth: "And as he passed by, he saw Levi the son of Alphaeus sitting at the tax booth, and he said to him, 'Follow me.' And he rose and followed him" (Mark 2:14). Peter and Andrew left their nets; James and John left their father in the boat![4] Livelihood, security, family, plans, and comforts are all on the chopping block for the one who would follow Jesus. To remove all ambiguity, Jesus stated it clearly: "And he said to all, 'If anyone would come after me, let him deny himself and take up his cross daily and follow me. For whoever would save his life will lose it, but whoever loses his life for my sake will save it'" (Luke 9:23–24).

From the beginning of Christ's ministry, discipleship was as much about following Jesus as it was forsaking the world. John Stott describes discipleship as a "radical nonconformity to the surrounding culture."[5] This radical nonconformity is the reverse side of the Christian's radical conformity to Christ. "There are no disciples of Jesus who are not following Jesus," writes Mark Dever, further explaining to today's disciples, "You no longer set the agenda for your own life; Jesus Christ does that. You belong to him now."[6] Those who belong to Christ quickly discover they must also help others follow our Lord: disciples disciple. "Part of our obedience," Dever adds, "is leading others to obedience."[7]

Making disciples, the key element of the Great Commission—and thus the church's mission—involves both evangelism and discipleship. Robby Gallaty states, "Evangelism is embedded within the discipleship process."[8] Disciple-making is leading people both to saving faith in Christ and toward ever-increasing conformity to His will. This is why Jesus explains that making disciples involves both baptizing people (the outward expression of placing faith in Christ) and teaching them to observe His commands. The sustained success of both evangelism and discipleship is found when they operate in concert.

The Lukewarm Church

The evangelism and discipleship just described often appear suited only for elite Christians, those believers who have received a special ability poured out by God's Spirit to pursue Christ and His mission. While some will experience a special manifestation of God's grace, the Bible describes discipleship and evangelism as normal practices for every believer. Bill Hull agrees when he writes,

> Is the need for disciple making limited to a few overzealous souls? Should evangelistic organizations and small church committees take on the whole task of evangelizing the world? What place does discipling have in the contemporary church? Somewhat ironically, to return it to the Great Commission, today's church has required a radical movement with the sole purpose of returning itself to a serious commitment to making disciples, as Christ commanded.[9]

Every believer is called to follow Christ while inviting others to do the same.

But this is not the typical experience in churches today. Not every believer fully embraces vibrant discipleship and evangelism. We might expect at least half of Christians to engage actively in these practices. Sadly, that is not the case. In 2012, Lifeway Research discovered that eighty percent of evangelical Christians acknowledged a personal responsibility to share their faith, but only thirty-nine percent had done so in the prior six months.[10] Fifty-six percent of Christians reported that they did not share their faith in the past year.[11] Consider: according to a 2018 Barna survey, nearly half of practicing Christian millennials seem to think evangelism is wrong![12] Those who do share, however, experience greater confidence in their own faith. Nearly nine out of ten of these find their faith strengthened.[13] Evangelism strengthens discipleship. If the devil can prevent our sharing, he can stunt our growth.

There's more unwelcome news. Discipleship efforts are lesser than Scripture indicates they should be. Churches have reported forty-four percent of their members are involved in regular discipleship in 2022, down from fifty percent in 2008.[14] When surveying Christians themselves, Barna found even less promising results. Only one in three practicing Christians agreed that studying the Bible with a group is at least somewhat important, and only one in five are involved in any discipleship activity with someone else.[15] Christians who do not actively grow in their faith are less inclined to share it with others. Stunted growth snuffs out sharing.

Several factors contribute to these revealing statistics. Though believers are new creations in Christ with God's Spirit in them, all Christians are tempted to return to sinful living. This is not a new problem. The New Testament writers admonished the earliest Christians with these words: "Beloved, I urge you as sojourners and exiles to abstain from the passions of the flesh, which wage war against your soul" (1 Pet. 2:11). The struggle Peter identifies challenges all believers; it magnifies the need for church leaders to ask themselves if their means of discipleship are adequately adjuring their people to the radical abandonment of the world and the wholehearted embracing of Christ. In most cases, a church's disciple-making efforts need improving.

The essential problem in the modern disciple-making process may be the separation of discipleship from evangelism. God designed the DNA of the church to be a combined double helix for a powerful impact that cannot operate with its parts working independently. Too often, discipleship reverts to education, and evangelism reverts to outreach. Each of these can have an impact on its own, but neither is sustainable in isolation. On their own, the result resembles that of poor farming practices: mediocre instead of thriving growth.

Discipleship Reverts to Education

The desired dynamic spiritual growth described in God's Word cannot be sustained by merely attending a program. Programs thrive on order, stability, and predictability, whereas Spirit-filled growth is spontaneous and unpredictable.[16] On its own, any discipleship program or prolonged effort will revert to increasingly stable and inert versions of what it was before, like certain elements on the periodic table. You may recall these from your chemistry class. For example, plutonium—an element able to power nuclear reactors—will on its own decay into lead. The element known as *discipleship* can decay into a more stable element that is a poor reflection of its former potency. Vibrant discipleship programs revert to education that emphasizes information over transformation.

Evangelism Reverts to Outreach

While outreach does not necessarily imply poor intent, its use here refers to a church's efforts that lack the power of more direct approaches—efforts that are a more settled, sterile version of what they were designed to be. Yet the power of these programs is found not in their predictable aspects but in the Holy Spirit, who guides people to make disciples.

The growth of the early church was so explosive that unbelievers accused Christians of having turned the world upside down.[17] This radical upheaval came not from simple, initial prayers of faith in Christ but by the subsequent lifestyle shift as people began to follow His teaching. People who are led by the Holy Spirit and who focus others' attention on pursuing Christ unleash dynamic disciple-making.

On the other hand, evangelistic programs can easily degrade into something less dynamic.

People, too, can struggle with maintaining evangelistic fervor. They allow the powerful witness of evangelism to decompose to something more stable, less volatile—and far less life-changing.

Restoring a Vibrant Church

In His wisdom, God developed a means to sustain both discipleship and evangelism at their maximum potencies. Evangelism prevents the decay of discipleship, which in turn prevents the decay of evangelism. Disciple-making is the combination of these twin ministry endeavors. Its stability depends on the power of God and the clarity of enthusiastic people, but it in turn furthers evangelism and maintains vibrant spiritual growth.

Separation

Sadly, many couples—Christian couples, even—find their marriages dissolving in divorce. Some marriages telegraph hardship from the outset; others are like sucker punches that come when people who appeared to be the strongest throw in the marital towel. Regardless, virtually all broken marriages have one thing in common: their end was not so much a sudden event as it was an unconscious drift.

Churches drift, too. A great outreach program can develop such an importance within itself that those serving drift from their disciple-making purpose. This is seldom the result of a conscious choice but rather the result of a series of smaller choices that subconsciously elevate the program as the end rather than the means to discipleship. The program becomes a mission within itself instead of part of the mission to make disciples.

In Revelation 2, Christ's message to the church at Ephesus is that, though they held to the fundamental truths, they had left their first love. When a discipleship program becomes the objective in and of itself, repeating the drift of the Ephesus experience seems inevitable. God does not simply want His children to check theological boxes or measure themselves against behavioral standards. That puts them in pharisee territory. Absent from such a perfunctory version of Christianity is the heartfelt desire to stay true to the love of Christ. In other words, church members are in danger of going through the motions without maintaining a passion for the lost.

Restoration

If this sounds familiar to where you find yourself today, do not lose heart. God has restored many marriages to their vibrant start. By intentionally merging closer, couples have erased the unconscious drift. Hurts have been forgiven, hearts have been mended, and homes have again become beacons of hope for others. The same is true with the bride of Christ. Although the drift can lead to lukewarm mediocrity, many churches have experienced renewal. Use the following questions to assess where you are and where God wants to draw you.

Questions to Consider

How do you diagnose mission drift? Asking insightful questions can reveal the drift within each program or ministry:

1. How do each of the ministry's volunteers define success for that ministry?
2. What evaluation questions does the ministry ask to assess its own success?

3. How well does the ministry connect with other discipleship ministries in your church? How well does it connect its participants with others in other ministries?

4. To what extent does the outreach ministry attempt to help people take the next spiritual step? Is that next step defined?

5. Which matters more: the number of people involved or the percentage of people who are taking the next spiritual steps?

CHAPTER 4

RECOVERING A DISCIPLE-MAKING MINDSET

Rogue Sprouts and Surprise Recoveries

The plant-health farmers eventually became known as greenhouse farmers. They toiled with brilliant success. Any soil that stayed at the farm after coming for an ant event was potted and placed in one of the climate-controlled greenhouses. Most often, the soil already had a plant growing that needed tending. Staking and pruning were routine tasks for the greenhouse farmers, who wanted each plant to have the perfect appearance. This, of course, provided the plant with better self-esteem.

Ironically, many well-tended plants seemed to worry more about their appearance and health than those that had never been treated. Were their branches symmetrical? Did their leaves hold uniform color and shape? Shouldn't they be flowering by now? The greenhouse farmers helped these plants, who relied on their competent care.

The greenhouse farmers added fertilizer to treat the soil. The brand of fertilizer chosen was well-known for promoting vibrant blooms that lasted a long time—so long, in fact, that the blooms rarely progressed to fruit development. No one seemed to mind because the plants had become so attractive, and many farmers now purchased their seed from a catalog rather than gather it from the harvest.

But not all plants handled their treatment well. The modern versions of indoor plants proved more delicate than their outdoor counterparts of the past. Some were fragile and failed to thrive even in their controlled environment. Those that did not make it were put on the compost pile. It was a sad development, but the farmers understood this to be a part of farming in a difficult world. Sometimes a plant was taken to the pile while sick so that it could live out its final days outdoors.

One day, a farmer removed a sickly plant and carried it to the compost pile. That same day, another farmer was cleaning out a storage area and discovered some seeds that they no longer used. These were varieties that had been harvested from plants several seasons ago. With a sweep of his hand, the farmer scattered the forgotten seed on the compost pile.

A month later, the same two farmers were making the trek to the compost pile, and what they saw amazed them. Plants were growing in the pile! These were not just any plants (weeds often crept in when the pile had not been turned). These plants were healthy farm plants. The farmers were at a loss to explain how this had happened, until one of them noticed the formerly sick plant he had placed there. Against all expectation, the plant had rebounded, driving its roots into the nutrient-rich compost, and sending new growth upward. The other farmer then remembered that he had tossed the forgotten seeds onto the pile the same day.

These farmers gathered the others, who also marveled at the sight. What could it mean? They recalled the days some of the older farmers had described when seed was scattered on the soil. They reminisced about the evolution of farming: the opposition to seed scattering, the focus on soil, and the change in farming philosophy. Who would have thought plants could still grow outside of the greenhouse?

The farmers held an emergency meeting to discuss the matter further. Plans for a newer and better greenhouse had already been in the works; it included several individual rooms at the rear with excellent views and even more state-of-the-art technology to tend the plants. The front of the building was an auditorium with a stage specifically designed for ant activities, with seating designed for pots of all sizes. Not a bad seat could be found. The building, however, was to be built on the most prominent field on the farm, and adjoining fields would be paved for parking. The farmers now found themselves reconsidering the endeavor.

"Stick with the plan," argued some. "Finding a few rogue sprouts in a pile out back does not change what we have known for decades. Outdoor planting will not work."

"Simply delay the plan while we try moving our operations outdoors for a spell," others contended. "If our farming practices can look more like what the Master

Gardener showed us, we should try outdoor planting again."

Back and forth each side argued its position. Eventually, they determined to try planting outdoors and to move forward with the new building only if the rediscovered technique failed. So began their project to restore the fields for growing crops, and with it came a new sense of adventure—one that would require tremendous effort and perseverance.

Principle #4: Mission fruitfulness is achieved only when people both see it and seek it from God.

Becoming Restless

Thus far we have established that God's Word and salvation through Christ alone combine to form the only foundation for disciple-making in the church and that all church activities should reflect the Great Commission. We have seen that well-meaning churches have unintentionally obscured (or even obstructed) their missions through programmatic clutter, which, despite bearing some fruit, often required pruning. We have also noted that separating discipleship and evangelism reduces their respective effectiveness and leads to decay over time. Thus, while the church has experienced external resistance toward making disciples, the church's internal practices have contributed to the problem, too. Francis Chan describes ignoring these issues: "Week after week, the same faces show up with little to no change in their lives. Insanely, we just keep doing the same thing, hoping it will yield different results."[18]

The mechanisms that would produce change require a sense of dissatisfaction with the status quo. As culture changes, churches must discern how to apply the timeless truths from God's Word to the changes in culture around them. Diminishing returns on ministry investment are the chief indicator and primary motivator to reconsider how best to make disciples. Eric Geiger and Kevin Peck challenge leaders, "Do you really want a church that is growing in unity and toward maturity? Then make your cause, your holy cause, the equipping and preparing of God's people. The epidemic of unhealthy churches is the result of churches and church leaders being woefully undercommitted to equipping people for the ministry and the mission of God."[19] Until a church becomes restless with the status quo and desires to see change, there will not be enough motivation to effect that change. John Piper emphasizes this God-ordained dissatisfaction, stating, "It is unthinkable that we should be content with things the way they are in a fallen world and an imperfect church. Therefore, God has been pleased to put a holy restlessness into some of his people, and those people will very likely be the leaders."[20] Churches must become dissatisfied if they are to embrace necessary change.

Becoming Dependent

The longing for a return to vibrancy can lead a church to experience renewal. The prophet Joel describes a similar feeling among God's people who had grown callous to spiritual things. Their agrarian society in Joel's day had fallen on hard times; the days of plenty were long behind them. Additionally, a series of calamities had befallen them: droughts, fires, and waves of locusts. When the people were desperate, they assembled to cry out for the Lord's help. The priests publicly offered a plea to God. After seeking God's mercy, they appealed to God's glory. They asked that other nations would see the evidence of God at work among His people. Following their petition, God intervened on their behalf.

God Alone Brings Change

God deliberately waited until His people were so fed up with the current state of things—desperate, actually—that they called a solemn assembly of young and old. Then He stepped in to bring relief. Now that the people were despondent and dejected, they were ready to rely wholly on God rather than on their own strength. God's response to His children includes these words:

> I will restore to you the years that the swarming locust has eaten, the hopper, the destroyer, and the cutter, my great army, which I sent among you. You shall eat in plenty and be satisfied, and praise the name of the LORD your God, who has dealt wondrously with you. And my people shall never again be put to shame. You shall know that I am in the midst of Israel, and that I am the LORD your God and there is none else. And my people shall never again be put to shame. (Joel 2:25–27)

Restoration emerges from desperation. When circumstances move people to depend wholly on God, they will find Him ready to act on their behalf. Consider the hopelessness of the nation of Israel when led to the banks of the Red Sea: God arranged their circumstances to yield a fevered pitch of despair. Israel saw the clouds of dust rising in the distance, kicked up by Pharaoh's army speeding toward them. Dust like that could also have been kicked up had God determined to open the earth and swallow the enemy army (a sign that God later performed). Had God used the earth in that way at that moment, Israel would not have feared the Egyptians but instead received a report of God's rescue. God pursued an alternate approach: allow Israel to be pushed to extreme anguish so that they could see His deliverance.

God alone can provide fruit in your church. He is not limited by imperfect people or their incomplete methods. Hearts aligned with His heart and voices crying out to Him present no opportunity for an army to stand in the way of His vibrant and vigorous bride. Regardless of the barriers in your church's present situation, God can bless with abundant fruit right in front of your eyes. Such abundance, however, seems to come when we, God's people, rely solely on God's deliverance—not our own efforts done our own way.

Seeking God's Favor

Because God alone can bring change, His children must seek His favor. Earthly parents love their children, yet they are not always favorably disposed to comply with their every request (often for good reason). In some cases, favor is withheld so that a child can experience natural consequences and learn from mistakes. In other cases, favor is granted in one area because a child has shown growth in another. God's children should seek the favor of their heavenly Father. In Psalm 90, Moses prays these words: "Let the favor of the LORD our God be upon us, and establish the work of our hands upon us; yes, establish the work of our hands!" (Ps. 90:17).

When we ask for His hand of favor to do His will, there is nothing manipulative or prosperity-driven about acknowledging that our efforts are futile without Him. Admittedly, in modern Christianity, "name it and claim it" theology has polluted that well. However, that is not what the Scriptures teach when the psalmist petitions God with these words: "I entreat your favor with all my heart; be gracious to me according to your promise" (Ps. 119:58). As God's children, we are invited to seek His gracious support in these things. We are reminded in Hebrews, "Let us then with confidence draw near to the throne of grace, that we may receive mercy and find grace to help in time of need" (Heb. 4:16). The recovery of a disciple-making, churchwide mindset will begin when a few humbly seek for His favor and grace among His people.

Visualize

People may be dissatisfied with the status quo, but they will never embrace what could be unless they can visualize it. In other words, as ineffective as the familiar may be, Christians will often cling to a failed program until they can see the promise of what God is calling them to. Giving people examples of dynamic disciple-making may help them visualize the possibilities. Look for what is successful, however small, and then draw attention to it. Highlight every instance of people coming to faith or growing as disciples. Then discuss what factors helped make it happen. Seek to understand and share how that success can be repeated in others.

You may need to create examples that people can see. This could involve starting a new Bible study or refocusing an existing one to be more resolute regarding evangelism and discipleship. It may mean infusing an outreach with more tangible methods to help people develop their faith or become connected to the church. Sometimes God calls a person to be the lone example who helps people see not only what is possible but also what they are called to do.

Elijah is a classic example. He found himself alone on Mount Carmel. He was not alone numerically; thousands had gathered. But he stood alone as one who feared God, and he squared off against 450 prophets of the false god, Baal. In this showdown, the frenetic efforts of the false prophets brought no response from Baal, yet the people were not willing to return to the one true God. They could not, or would not, visualize His power. Then Elijah called out to God, and the Lord answered this man's prayer by sending a flaming ball of fire to consume Elijah's sacrifice! The people saw and proclaimed, "The Lord, he is God!" (1 Kings 18:39).

God still uses small groups of faithful people—even lone individuals—to help people see God and His power. In this way, people learn to follow Him. Those who step out in faith can become the examples that turn hearts toward healthy disciple-making to the glory of God.

Sometimes, God raises up the next generation to help people see the possibility of renewal. Many churches find themselves wishing they still had the dynamic ministry of the prior decade. It may be we have not incorporated younger people into the leadership and main body of ministry. Ministry leaders must find ways to cultivate younger people to step into key roles. Robby Gallaty observes,

> It is worth challenging our cultural norms here. Perhaps we should consider entrusting younger men and women with ministerial duties. Some of the ripest believers for discipleship may be younger adults who are in this stage of life: moldable,

shapeable, flexible, and available with a future discipleship ministry of many years still ahead of them.[21]

An example in Scripture: Moses incorporated younger men to offer burnt offerings when the people bound themselves to God's covenant.[22] Young people often rise to the occasion when entrusted with leadership responsibilities, and such investments bring ministry dividends that extend to future generations.

God also uses newer members as a rich source of fresh perspective. They are less tied to aspects of a ministry that may have become cultural relics, putting them in a better position to visualize opportunities for increased ministry vibrancy. People in leadership often hang on to their roles, little realizing that renewed growth might occur if those newer to the church were given space to join in ministry and leadership. Leadership rotation can prevent decay. It may also prevent bitterness when leaders who have carried the burden for so long wonder why no one is willing to take up the mantle. Programs can become energized when space is allowed for others to carry on the work of disciple-making.

Mindset Recovery

The recovery of a disciple-making mindset can occur when people are reminded of what is not only possible but even commanded by Christ. Leaders often understand this call but are uncertain how to effect change amid the hectic clutter of ministry. Understanding the interrelationship between discipleship and evangelism, and finding examples where they dynamically occur, may help people glimpse where God is leading the ministry. Only by relying on God can true change occur.

While God is the source of all change, He operates through the hands and feet of His people. Unsurprisingly, this requires believers who seek to carry out all that God has called them to do. Part Two of this book will offer guidance on how to take effective and lasting steps to align a church or ministry with its mission to make disciples.

Questions to Consider

1. What behaviors—personally and as a group—demonstrate dependence on God to bring change?

2. What examples does your church have of people embracing dynamic discipleship? Effective evangelism? Both combined?

3. What factors have contributed to the success of these examples?

4. How can these examples help others see the possibility of increased ministry fruitfulness?

5. How easy is it for young or new people to find meaningful roles in your ministry or church?

PART TWO

Restoring the Mission
of the Church

CHAPTER 5

DEVELOP THE MISSION

Garden Plots

Encouraged by the newfound growth and production from plants, the farmers considered how best to develop their farm to accommodate increased seed sowing. Initially, they began simply to move plants outdoors, assuming the plants would immediately flourish and produce like they had so long ago. They quickly discovered, however, that the plants would need much more care. Some of the farmers strategized how to help these plants thrive.

They remembered the Master Gardener's teaching about sowing seed and understanding soil types. This was already familiar to them, for they had written it down, but they had been interpreting the words differently. The teaching on the soil types had guided them when they ordered good potting soil for the greenhouse. Now, with dirt under their fingernails, they saw just how varied the ground could be.

The farmers considered their climate and topography. One farmer, who mostly worked with younger plants, chose a patch of land to till for these tender shoots, ensuring every hindering stone was removed and providing bright canopies above to shield from the harshest periods of sun. Another farmer who worked with more mature plants determined to transplant them on a terraced and rolling hillside. This provided an exquisite view of the farm, and the breeze cascading down the hill was a refreshing treat. Still another farmer began preparing a choice area of ground for some tall, reedy plants. When high winds came through and rushed among the plants, it whistled, producing delightful sounds that made all on the farm smile and give thanks for the wisdom of the Master Gardener.

But the farmers also encountered problems in these endeavors. In their haste to apply their new understanding to benefit their plants, they failed to collaborate. Consequently, some farmers were left with scrappy patches. Others found themselves in charge of more plants than their space allotment could sustain. These plants were crowded, which stunted their growth and left those farmers feeling inferior.

Even the plants themselves struggled. Instead of being progressively exposed to increasing time outdoors to develop hardiness, many plants were rushed from the greenhouse straight to the field. This shock caused many to wilt. In time, the high morale amongst the thriving plants made them question the low morale among the struggling plants. "Perhaps they need to work harder or be more adaptable to change," the strong ones mused. So, even the plants disagreed about the change in plans. The struggles among plants and farmers alike grew so *strong that many of them questioned their decision to adopt this new, outdoor endeavor. Perhaps it was an outdated model after all.*

Finally, the farmers came together to discuss the situation. One of them brought a map of their property to discuss how they could collaborate on the next planting season for the good of the entire farm. Another showed the weather patterns for their climate to help decide where to plant specific crops and what varieties of seed would work best. One particularly plucky farmer had learned of another farm in the area who had made similar changes a few years prior. The farmers there had proved a wealth of knowledge, and some of their painful experiences had taught them lessons that could help these farmers.

They had even discovered ways to nurture their plants to get them used to the new, outdoor settings. Because the most pressing need was helping more plants thrive, the farmers developed not only the best plans to use their farm wisely but also the most effective ways to help plants enjoy the change.

Principle #5: A shared sense of mission must be collectively embraced to succeed.

Set the Direction

Once church leaders embrace a disciple-making mindset, they must help develop that mindset among the church members. The local church is not a building or a set of programs or a pastoral staff. It is a body of believers who are called to follow Christ. God calls leaders to present a clear mission that the rest of the body can comprehend. These leaders set the direction of the church by convincing people to adopt a set of practices to accomplish a set of goals. Those goals, in turn, reflect faithfulness to the mission set forth by God to lead people to trust in and follow Christ.

Many worthy, mission-minded endeavors have ended in a whimper soon after beginning because the leaders did not communicate important mission factors. Leaders will do well to establish the right mission, expand a widespread mindset among the people, and ensure practical methods are employed. Understanding and incorporating these three factors are crucial for mission success.

The Right Mission

A well-crafted mission creates a clear picture of where the church is headed. Leaders must imagine the future state in enough detail to display it vividly so their people in turn can envision it. For that mission to be true to God's Word, it must reflect the Great Commission's command to make disciples. Furthermore, that mission should reflect a specific call from God.

The book of Acts chronicles the spread of the gospel as disciples are made in ever-widening geographical regions of the Roman Empire. Until persecution began, the believers mostly remained in Jerusalem. When persecution scattered them, they shared the gospel and made disciples.

Acts 13 describes the first call to travel for the express purpose of sharing the gospel abroad. Recount with me the story of this missionary effort: "While they were worshiping the Lord and fasting, the Holy Spirit said, 'Set apart for me Barnabas and Saul for the work to which I have called them.'

Then after fasting and praying they laid their hands on them and sent them off" (Acts 13:2–3). This successful missionary journey leads to another, in which Paul, already knowing the will of the Spirit, decides to travel again to strengthen the churches. Read the words and imagine the excitement that was spreading in the early church: "And after some days Paul said to Barnabas, 'Let us return and visit the brothers in every city where we proclaimed the word of the Lord, and see how they are'" (Acts 15:36). While on this journey, Paul considers sharing the gospel in new regions, and the call of the Holy Spirit again comes into play:

> And they went through the region of Phrygia and Galatia, having been forbidden by the Holy Spirit to speak the word in Asia. And when they had come up to Mysia, they attempted to go into Bithynia, but the Spirit of Jesus did not allow them. So, passing by Mysia, they went down to Troas. And a vision appeared to Paul in the night: a man of Macedonia was standing there, urging him and saying, "Come over to Macedonia and help us." And when Paul had seen the vision, immediately we sought to go on into Macedonia, concluding that God had called us to preach the gospel to them. (Acts 16:6–10)

The Holy Spirit clarified the disciple-making mission of a church with a more specific disciple-making call to a specific congregation in Antioch. They were found fasting and seeking God when the Spirit set Paul and Barnabas apart for the first missionary journey. The Lord had called them in their present discipling endeavors, and He enhanced their calling during a time when they were earnestly seeking Him.

We can learn from their experience. Our discipline initiatives should start with the Great Commission: "Go therefore and make disciples of all nations, baptizing them in the name of the Father and of the Son and of the Holy Spirit, teaching them to observe all that I have commanded you. And behold, I am with you always, to the end of the age" (Matt. 28:19–20).

A church will find itself on the right mission whenever its efforts are centered on making disciples. We do not need to wait for a special call to disciple people. Jesus Christ called all believers to this ministry just before He ascended into heaven. Any extensions or additions to the original mission of the church will be directly tied to the Great Commission. In the case of Paul and Barnabas, the Spirit directed them to a new location, Macedonia, where different people awaited the good news. Similarly, a church may discover a particular calling that relates to their region or audience.

Leaders must discern what God is calling the church to do before leading people to pursue a mission. God has given every church an exciting call to spread the gospel through the existing members and among the community where He has placed them. The particulars of that call require the discernment of leaders who seek God's wisdom and direction. In the hectic busyness of ministry, church leaders may find themselves proposing a mission of their own thinking rather than from the Holy Spirit's guidance. A church will find her efforts frustrated and her resources scarce when energy is siphoned away from what God has called her to accomplish.

Another lesson comes from Paul and Barnabas's experience. A more specific calling will sometimes be discovered through supplication or circumstances. The apostles were actively seeking God through worship and fasting when the Spirit directed their mission. The same dynamic happened later to Paul and Silas. They were actively serving when the Spirit used circumstances to guide them toward a new mission field. Whether quietly seeking or actively serving, the Spirit uses direct or circumstantial means to make His will known.

As the Lord communicates the discipleship ministry in a specific direction, leaders must dwell on God's direction, praying over it and considering its implications. They must seek counsel, talking with people to gain wise perspectives and feedback. They must consider how best to communicate the mission and how it ties in with the Great Commission. One thing is certain: if this is the right mission, it will clearly reflect God's call to discipleship; leaders then establish objectives to pursue along the way.

Mindset and Timing

While the leaders in a church are members who serve with faithfulness and humility, a dichotomy exists between the leaders and the members, sometimes described as the clergy and the laity. If leaders struggle to impart to others the passion they feel toward an endeavor, some will follow with apathy or minimal tolerance, while others may be openly hostile. Sometimes the problem rests in the past, leaving the people hesitant. This may be the umpteenth shiny new endeavor they have been asked to support. In other words, confidence in church leaders may be low.

No matter how good the mission sounds, a church without a motivating mindset may lack the will to pursue it. Like a plane without fuel sitting on the runway, a church without a mission mindset cannot generate lift to achieve takeoff. Sadly, many churches with a good missions ministry taxi along the runway but never get airborne. We could apply a lesson from aviation: planes are fueled long before they ever reach the runway.

If a mission does not fire up the flight crew, it will lack sufficient thrust to carry it aloft. Let me state it differently: mission must embed itself within the culture of a church. Nehemiah was burdened to repair the wall of Jerusalem for eight months before he made his request to the king. Once the king bought in, Nehemiah traveled to Jerusalem and waited before presenting his vision to the people. After riding out to inspect the ruins around the city, Nehemiah describes what happened next:

> And the officials did not know where I had gone or what I was doing, and I had not yet told the Jews, the priests, the nobles, the officials, and the rest who were to do the work. Then I said to them, "You see the trouble we are in, how Jerusalem lies in ruins with its gates burned. Come, let us build the wall of Jerusalem, that we may no longer suffer derision." And I told them of the hand of my God that had been upon me for good, and also of the words that the king had spoken to me. And they said, "Let us rise up and build." So they strengthened their hands for the good work. (Neh. 2:16–18)

In Nehemiah's case, the people subscribed to his plan after he explained the problem and the solution: God's favor was upon them to restore the wall. When a leader can credibly communicate both the problem and the plan, people are far more likely to join the mission. Wise leaders will await God's timing and then communicate a clear objective.

The bigger the mission, the more people want to see the potential for success. In the God-ordained mission of the church, people want to sense God's guiding hand. Had Nehemiah defected from the king and stolen away to Jerusalem, he could have arrived sooner, but the people may not have been moved to respond. Wait on God's timing—and pray for the people to adopt a mission mindset.

Practical Methods

A powerful mission, even if adopted by the people, may not be effective if there is no execution plan. If the mission is the destination, and the mindset is the willingness of the people to go, the methods will answer the question, "How will we get there?" The methods are like the mode of travel, including the markers along the way. Thinking through this critical portion of the plan will keep a mission from waning.

Sometimes the leaders are gun-shy, hesitant to champion a new endeavor because of failures in their past. They know the people had subscribed wholeheartedly to a poorly planned past mission, and the leaders know the experience subsequently jaded them. By shepherding gently while relying God's power and timing, leaders can instill confidence in the Lord to again lead people to God's mission.

A wise leader will think through the specifics of a plan and guide his people through each step. Without practical methods, a mission is simply an aspiration. It requires prayer and planning. At this stage, a leader would do well to ask a few key individuals to pray together about the mission. God often works through the collaboration of others to bring a mission to fruition.

What Is Lacking?

Mission + Mindset – Methods = Frustration. A church that responds to a mission with a wholehearted mindset but lacks practical methods to execute may soon descend into frustration. One way to refine methods of the mission can be seen in the business world. Businesses often launch new products or services in targeted markets to test and revise the product before fully launching it. In other words, see what sticks in a "laboratory" of your church that is much smaller than the entire congregation. Like a chemist who observes and records measurements during experimentation, a faithful leader will note results to help people understand the "why" and "how" to replicate successful methods. Without well thought-out methods, volunteers may be hesitant even to try.

Mission + Methods – Mindset = Impotence. Leaders with the right mission and practical methods but without people of the same mindset may be frustrated by the lack of cohesion to implement effective change. Their toil will always be with too few people. But the fault may be at the leadership level: if they lacked patience or failed to communicate the vision, the people may not have bought in due to confusion, not rejection. If leaders move ahead to a difficult crossing with only the ablest few, they may find themselves wondering why the rest did not follow. Worse, if the leader expresses frustration or belittles the reluctant for their lack of involvement, the resulting wounds may never heal. Overcome pushback with effective communication.

Methods + Mindset – Mission = Apathy. People with a broadly positive mindset and operating with practical methods may nonetheless reap failure if they are perpetuating a worn-out mission. Perhaps the prior mission was adequate and led to success in an earlier season, but reasons abound to retire it today: it has not been trumpeted regularly; earlier successes have fallen into decline; techniques or personalities are driving the old mission rather than God, and so on. As positive results diminish, people can become frustrated from struggling with a mission that has grown less relevant. They may drift to other activities or find themselves blaming the next generation for the drift.

A leader and his team must refine the mission and vision when appropriate. He must ensure that each of the three critical components—mission, methods, and mindset—is in place. And the leader must work with his pastoral team to minimize blind spots by garnering inputs from various perspectives.

A Team Effort

Through a team, key people can help craft the direction and refine the mission. Group participation is vital to mission success. Within such a team, however, specific challenges can either help or distract from mission success. Perceiving the stages of implementation and addressing best practices in each will increase the likelihood of success.

While the mission is still aspirational, the leader should give prayerful consideration about whom to approach to assess and refine it. A small team of two to four people should be adequate. Avoid overplanning the mission before this stage; a leader who preplans all the details will likely fall in love with his vision and be resistant to change. He will answer probing questions as though he is defending a dissertation rather than considering other potential factors. The other members of the team may see this and realize their role was not to help plan but to provide a rubber stamp approval.

When a leader brings a few people into the planning process, the mission can be analyzed from several angles. The team can assess what needs to be accomplished to develop the vision. After this small group has refined the mission and the methods, they can present it to a larger group for further refinement. Depending on the size of your congregation, this step may be with a broader group of leaders and laity, or it may be the congregation as a whole.

Prayer and Resources

Plan Prayerfully. Because God is the source of your mission, continue to consult Him throughout the process. Any church can make plans, but only through prayer and sensitivity to the Holy Spirit's leading can a church clarify its mission. James warns against those who make plans to travel and turn a profit through business but do not consult God.[23] He goes as far as to call it boasting. This applies to churches that make plans without consulting God. God is not impressed by the quality of *our* plans. He is concerned with the condition of our hearts. Churches that make plans without consulting God exhibit spiritual impudence as they rely on their work rather than on God's will.

Jesus speaks of a day of judgment for those who based their identity on the great works they did for God while concurrently disobeying His will.[24] They will claim to have prophesied, done wonders, and even cast out demons in the name of Jesus—yet Jesus equates their activity with lawlessness and may utter, "I never knew you; depart from me" (Matt. 7:23). For all their well-meaning activities, these people did not do the will of the Father.

It is important to take time to wrestle over your mission with godly counselors. Be patient for God to guide and respond when He does. If the vision is not clear at this point, wait for God to make it clear. The result will be a mission that is from God rather than from men. As Scripture says, "Many are the plans in the mind of a man, but it is the purpose of the LORD that will stand" (Prov. 19:21).

Plan Resourcefully. To their delight, a team will discover that God has equipped them to enhance the mission He is calling them to fulfill. Consider how God has already provided resources your church can leverage. People tend to gravitate to the tangible—to what they can see and touch. Ask these questions:

- To whom among us has God given certain gifts, skills, and experiences that can help accomplish the mission?

- Where has God placed our church geographically to help refine our mission? If your church is not tied to a single location, can this be advantageous to the mission?

- What facilities or materials has God already provided to help accomplish the mission?

- What does the church have that the community wants or needs? For instance, classroom space for an English as a Second Language ministry or gym space for athletics might be used strategically to further the mission. Even the parking lot could be the site of a community yard sale or hot rod show. When these activities are aligned with the mission, a church can leverage them to bear significant fruit.

Plan Creatively. A church must consider not only its advantages but also its challenges. The mission is not simply about following the path of least resistance; it is about accomplishing

God's calling, which may involve significant obstacles. Highway planners often follow the natural path of the land for a new roadway, but they have also been known to blast through mountains. Prayerfully determine if a barrier needs to be removed, or merely avoided, for the sake of the mission.

Handling Opposition

Opposition to the mission will always arise. Moses, David, Nehemiah, Paul, and Jesus all experienced opposition. Their fortitude was tied to the source of their mission: God and His will. If a leader is not convinced that a mission is God-given, that leader will lack the conviction to withstand opposition. A wise leader will trace God's hand in the development of the mission, drawing others in to confirm the same. This frees a leader to pursue God's will instead of the whims of anyone else.

Get ready: people will critique your mission for assorted reasons. Some are comfortable with the status quo or resistant to change, while others want to test the resolve of the leaders before committing wholeheartedly to its execution. Some may perceive genuine issues that, if addressed properly, will strengthen your success. Lean into the opposition—consider them an opportunity. View critics as future partners. Within each challenge there is the possibility that you may win others' hearts to the mission God has laid on your heart.

Many biblical examples exist to guide you as a leader who is advancing a God-given mission. Reflect on how the Lord changed the heart of Saul, transforming him into the Apostle Paul. This man was on a personal mission to oppose the church; he persecuted Christians by imprisoning and even killing them. God intervened and changed Saul's heart. And in the case of the Old Testament Saul—the first king of

Israel—we also find a man in opposition to God's will. God intervened in his life too: not by changing the king's heart but by removing him altogether. Pray for God to intercede in the "Sauls" of your congregation. It is a joy when their opposition ceases and they dramatically turn around; less joyful, but still to His glory, is when God's providence removes the defiance of the recalcitrant from your congregation.

In the Old Testament, Gideon had no reason to doubt the mission: an angel demonstrated God's power while delivering it! Yet Gideon was fearful: he struggled to implement it before receiving further signs that God was at work. You may have Gideons in your church. Give them space to see examples of mission success. They may soon boldly lead the charge.

How about Moses—a man with a checkered past, one marked with failure from his prior attempt at the mission? He put up several objections before submitting to God. Some people, like Moses, do not want to repeat the mistakes of the past, so they resolve not to get involved unless they have clearly and directly heard from God that they should.

In the New Testament, Nicodemus did not buy into to Jesus's mission right away. He had genuine questions that, once answered, eventually convinced him. He never became the most active proponent of the mission, but he played a key role in a portion of it. Give people the space to be like Nicodemus. Some will ask questions and seem to sit on the sidelines, but later they may provide support in a particularly challenging phase.

Leaders will thankfully encounter some Rahabs and Ruths who immediately get involved however they can. They will have a few Peters, whose clumsy enthusiasm sometimes seems like a liability. They will even find that those originally in opposition to the mission will be more effective than some of the early proponents. Jesus told a parable of two sons whose father told them to work in the vineyard: the son who verbally agreed never went to work, while the initially defiant son was the one who obeyed (Matt. 21:28–32).

Patience is paramount as leaders consider what encouragement or motivation certain individuals need most. Paul, with Silvanus and Timothy, urged Christians to "admonish the idle, encourage the fainthearted, help the weak, be patient with them all" (1 Thess. 5:14). Christlike patience wins the day because God is the One who works in the hearts of people. Patiently give God's Spirit room to work in them.

Questions to Consider

A church must develop the right mission with a broadly agreed mindset and practical methods.

1. Which of these elements is strongest within your church: mission, mindset, or methods?
2. How can you increase the strength of the weakest of the three?
3. What role is prayer playing in the planning and execution of your church's mission? How is this apparent?
4. How can the unique resources in your church be used to accomplish the mission?
5. Who may require special attention to be lovingly coaxed toward embracing the mission?

CHAPTER 6

RECRUIT BY THE MISSION

Farmer Turnover

Not all farmers were convinced of the changed strategy. The ant farmers saw little relationship between their role and the location of plant growth. They did not mind the changes but believed their responsibilities exempted them from involvement. Whether the plants grew outdoors or in a greenhouse, the role of the ant farmers had not changed. However, some farmers in the greenhouse were hostile to the change, and they were not without arguments to bolster their resistance.

Because several of the plants had initially been rushed out of the greenhouse, they wilted, and the angry farmers declared it a sign of a failed strategy. Though the other farmers explained the need to transition plants properly, the protestations persisted. With them came a litany of complaints disguised as helpful reminders about the virtues of greenhouse-only gardening.

"Sorry about your weed problem," one greenhouse farmer consoled. "Would you like help transplanting some of these plants back to the greenhouse? It is a weed-free environment!"

"The way you toil outdoors is impressive," remarked another. *"I could not imagine baking in the sun or even the stress on my back. The greenhouse shields me as I stand straight while tending the plants."*

Some commented that the plants were less ornate, while others pointed out the harmful pests plaguing the gardens. What had begun with an understanding that the greenhouses could extend the growing season for plants became a stream of explanations about why particular plants must remain there. Despite having collaborated on a clear plan, weeds of confusion had been sown with the seed.

The farmers gathered to discuss the matter. This time they reaffirmed the Master Gardener's instructions to scatter the seed and grow plants in fields, where those plants would produce a harvest that could also become future seed. The Master Gardener's objective had always been about plant growth and abundant harvest, not about plant beauty or farmer comfort.

Following the meeting, some farmers resigned to find another farm that suited their philosophy of farming. Although this diminished some of the conflict, a few plants and farmers still wondered if they were following the best plan. And a new problem arose: a labor shortage. The outdoor farm work was toilsome. Despite the conflict they had caused, the greenhouse farmers who left had nevertheless lightened the workload before their departure. The resignation of some ant farmers meant that plants more associated with ant activities felt less connected to the farm itself.

*The farmers erected help wanted signs, and different
farmers applied. The original farmers quickly realized
their need to hire only those who were willing to farm
according to the farm's plan. Some applicants affirmed
the farm's plan during their interviews but began to
propose the same farming ideas the farmers had recently
jettisoned. The most senior farmers valued quality farm
help—people who were committed to the farm's seed-
sowing mission.*

---

*Principle #6: Developing the right people
for the mission will preserve it from fracturing.*

Staff-Level Mission Unity

Cohesion matters. A church leader must unite his staff around
completing a singular mission. Yes, that mission comes from
Scripture, but the particulars—the local strategy and processes and opportunities—will vary in each local church.
Some staff may introduce adjustments to the mission, based
on their skills, personalities, and passions; other staff may
harm the mission by favoring an alternative, paying only lip
service to the mission at hand.

Who are the staff? Different churches define staff differently. For our purposes, *staff* refers to the primary champions
of a church's ministry efforts. The Bible lists specific character
and competence requirements for pastors (also called elders
or overseers) and deacons. One key passage is found in Paul's
first letter to Timothy:

The saying is trustworthy: If anyone aspires to the
office of overseer, he desires a noble task. Therefore

an overseer must be above reproach, the husband of one wife, sober-minded, self-controlled, respectable, hospitable, able to teach, not a drunkard, not violent but gentle, not quarrelsome, not a lover of money. He must manage his own household well, with all dignity keeping his children submissive, for if someone does not know how to manage his own household, how will he care for God's church? He must not be a recent convert, or he may become puffed up with conceit and fall into the condemnation of the devil. Moreover, he must be well thought of by outsiders, so that he may not fall into disgrace, into a snare of the devil. Deacons likewise must be dignified, not double-tongued, not addicted to much wine, not greedy for dishonest gain. They must hold the mystery of the faith with a clear conscience. And let them also be tested first; then let them serve as deacons if they prove themselves blameless. Their wives likewise must be dignified, not slanderers, but sober-minded, faithful in all things. Let deacons each be the husband of one wife, managing their children and their own households well. For those who serve well as deacons gain a good standing for themselves and also great confidence in the faith that is in Christ Jesus. (1 Tim. 3:1–13)

Many of these essential traits for pastors and deacons are likewise vital for other staff, including program directors, ministry leaders, or other leadership positions. Whether paid or volunteer, they are influential people in mission-critical positions.

When staff operate according to disparate missions, people notice the increased confusion. If staff are not aligned to the mission, they will lead others from it too. Their personal ministry priorities may even replace the mission, and those working nearby may unknowingly accommodate those mismatched priorities.

Some may object to this characterization. They may ask, "How bad can it be for a church to have staff leading in different ways as long as they are still leading people to God?" Remember that churches have limited resources and that God has called church leaders to steward those resources well, effectively leading people toward the mission set before them. Think of church leadership in terms of a team of horses harnessed to pull in the same direction. Arranging a harness at an odd angle will tax the entire team and slow its progress. Or picture it as the boosters in a rocket, arranged to propel the spacecraft away from the earth. If they are misaligned, it can spell disaster for the rocket. In other words, sideways energy, "drag" if you will, can impede the progress a church staff seeks to make toward the mission of making disciples.

Commitment over Compensation

When seeking to fill paid staff roles, a church would be wise to highlight the mission to which it is called. Great care should be exercised to recruit people who will be committed to the mission. Many churches seek to put together the right compensation and benefits package to attract a quality candidate. Amid the myriad details within such package, and in the calling or hiring process, the mission can sometimes be minimized. Interviews that include good questions about the mission will help reveal mission alignment. A quality candidate who is drawn to the church because of the mission is ideal.

In 1896, Booker T. Washington recruited George Washington Carver to come to the fledgling Tuskegee Institute by appealing to more than a mission, but a calling:

> I cannot offer you money, position, or fame. The first two you have. The last, from the place you now occupy, you will no doubt achieve. These things I now ask you to give up. I offer you in their place—work—hard, hard work—the challenge of bringing people from degradation, poverty and waste to full manhood.[25]

Carver, who indeed found himself in a prominent, well-paying position at Iowa State College, was moved by the mission. He set aside his lucrative position to struggle at Tuskegee and add agricultural training to the educational program for the poor student body of African American descent. Washington successfully tapped into the sense of mission Carver possessed. No salary negotiations took place. Carver simply replied that he would be there. In his reply, he wrote, "[I] shall be glad to cooperate with you in doing all I can through Christ who strengthened me to better the condition of our people."[26]

A wise leader who seeks a driven candidate will lead with the mission. This will allow him to find candidates similarly motivated. The ears of those who seek mission–level impact will perk up to the call. Scripture reminds us that a person who is "greedy for gain" (Titus 1:7b) is unqualified to be an overseer; instead, that person "must hold firm to the trustworthy word as taught" (Titus 1:9a). A person passionate about God's Word and mission will be attracted to a church that shares the same desires.

What about those compensation packages? Each church should do what it can to provide well for their paid leaders, as the Bible affirms. "Let the elders who rule well be considered worthy of double honor, especially those who labor in preaching and teaching. For the Scripture says, 'You shall not muzzle an ox when it treads out the grain,' and, 'The laborer deserves his wages'" (1 Tim. 5:17–18). Churches with fewer financial resources, however, should rest in the confidence that a God-inspired mission will see God-level provision. They will find others, like Carver, who are motivated more by God's mission than man's money.

Fit over Flashy

In the 2004 movie *Miracle*, Coach Herb Brooks (played by Kurt Russell) said, "I'm not looking for the best people. I'm looking for the right people." The film was based on the true story of the 1980 United States Olympic hockey team that overcame improbable odds to defeat their Soviet rivals and win the gold medal. Coach Brooks bypassed some of the most talented hockey players when assembling his ragtag team. The men he chose were not flashy, but they fit the team plan he had developed, and he knew that only players who fit his model could accomplish the mission of winning the gold. In the same way, churches must look for godly people who will fit the mission and paradigm of the church. Failing to do so will be detrimental to the church's unity and mission.

Look for Character. Recruiting for the mission involves rejecting candidates who seem to be qualified but are more flash than focus. The prophet Samuel learned this principle when God sent him to the house of Jesse to anoint Israel's next king. The prophet thought Jesse's oldest son, Eliab, was surely God's choice to be king, but God had other plans, saying, "Do not look on his appearance or on the height of his stature, because I have rejected him. For the LORD sees not as man sees: man looks on the outward appearance, but the LORD looks on the heart" (1 Sam. 16:7).

Searching for people of good character can be challenging. Some churches will seek indications of character on a job description but fail to ask probing questions in the interview process. A good leader will take time to consider how questions might be worded to gain a clear picture of a candidate's heart. Prayerfully ask God to reveal to you as He did to Samuel the person He has selected—and to identify those whom He has rejected. When the candidate comes from within the church, you may have already had an opportunity to know if that person is one after God's own heart. Let heartfelt devotion to Christ be a primary indicator of a worthy candidate.

Look for Competence. The church that has developed a disciple-making mission should seek someone who already makes disciples. This involves demonstrated competence. You should prefer a candidate who has made disciples over a candidate who *intends* to make disciples. For a pastor, this would involve someone who has already demonstrated both reaching and teaching priorities. A church may consider large-scale church outreaches to meet the reaching requirement, but outreach is best demonstrated at the relational level more than at the programmatic level. Teaching should yield spiritual growth geared toward making more disciples. Many effective pastors can lead a Bible study or craft a sermon, but these positions often call for an effective teacher who is also enthusiastic about leading people to Christ.

Paul found himself under scrutiny by the Corinthian believers. False teachers had come in while he was away, attempting to elevate themselves by disparaging him. They had apparently produced letters of reference about themselves and claimed that Paul's lack of references indicated his inferiority. Paul responded, "You yourselves are our letter of recommendation, written on our hearts, to be known and read by all. And you show that you are a letter from Christ delivered by us, written not with ink but with the Spirit of the living God, not on tablets of stone but on tablets of human hearts" (2 Cor. 3:2–3). Paul pointed to the lives he had impacted rather than a letter from a stranger. His point was that his competence had already been demonstrated in and among them. A qualified candidate should be able to point to changed lives as a testament of competence.

Look for Conduits. Competence and character take a person only so far. An ethical person with skill may do well in a secular job field, but the church relies on the power of God. Something greater than skill comes into play. This was famously acknowledged outside the church concerning the topic of warfare. Cardinal Mazarin, one of Italy's seventeenth-century chief ministers to France, declared, "One must not ask of a general, 'Is he skillful?' but rather 'Is he lucky?'"[27] His reasoning: when so many factors can change the course of a war, a lucky general is preferred over a merely skillful one.

What the world sees as luck Christians recognize as the invisible force of God's sovereignty working through a person. That person is a conduit, a demonstration of God's limitless power operating through a finite individual. Paul recognized his own limitations, without which he may have appeared to be more effective for Christ. But Paul understood that those limitations were a means for the power of Christ to work through him. He recounts his conversation this way: "But he said to me, 'My grace is sufficient for you, for my power is made perfect in weakness.' Therefore I will boast all the more gladly of my weaknesses, so that the power of Christ may rest upon me" (2 Cor. 12:9). Paul had gained a perspective we need to adopt.

Conduits are humble. Conduits are teachable. They recognize that they are not the total ministry package but are merely servants who do their part to make disciples and help others do the same. They understand that their power comes through God as they are empowered by His Spirit for ministry.

Look for Charisma. Many associate charisma with a dynamic, inspiring personality. The origin of *charisma* is Greek, meaning "favor" or "gift." In a qualified candidate, there should be found a sense of favor, of gifting. Timothy was charged to continue exercising his spiritual gifting, being told, "Practice these things, immerse yourself in them, so that all may see your progress" (1 Tim. 4:15). Jesus is described as One who increased in this favor: "And Jesus increased in wisdom and in stature and in favor with God and man" (Luke 2:52). A church leader should enjoy such favor; people should recognize this person as one worth following. A dynamic personality is not required; indeed, many qualified people would be missed if only the most dynamic people were chosen. But the leader worth following should have a reputation for following God. In that way, he will echo the Apostle Paul who urged, "Be imitators of me, as I am of Christ" (1 Cor. 11:1).

Look for Culture. The leader worth following will also be one who develops a good rapport with others. He may not be the most outgoing, but he must have a personality that is both personable and agreeable. Getting along with others and being likeable are essential traits for one called to impact lives. An aloof leader will be difficult to connect with and potentially hinder the disciple-making mission. Paul writes, "And the Lord's servant must not be quarrelsome but kind to everyone, able to teach, patiently enduring evil, correcting his opponents with gentleness" (2 Tim. 2:24–25). This kind, patient, and gentle spirit must be present.

The person should fit into the culture created by existing staff. If they do not mesh well, problems may arise, and the mission may be jeopardized. This will require another virtue: adaptability. Churches change and missions adjust over time. Staff members who adapt well to changes and challenges will be better able to adjust to the culture of the church.

Staff-Level Mission Clarity

A good leader will make his staff the primary recipients of mission communication. Sometimes a leader will communicate the mission to the congregation, assuming the staff are already aligned. He must be careful to make his staff the primary source of mission clarity, or confusion will be sown. It is critical to communicate with the volunteer staff as well. Good leaders reflect the character of a ministry in the clarity they provide to those who are part of the mission team.

Discuss the Mission

Build mission-related terms into your vocabulary. Language is a powerful tool that develops culture. Use words to describe both the existing situation and the desired reality. Sociologists understand language to be a core component around which groups and movements form. Many researchers, notes sociologist John Unseem, "describe the language of a group in order to identify its norms, predominant modes of behavior, and world views."[28] Ideas travel on the backs of words to influence thinking and reframe perspectives. When the staff speak in terms of the mission, they must develop clarity regarding its parts and concepts. As a leader, a large part of your job is to help every member embrace the mission—from your paid staff to your volunteers, from the oldest senior citizen to your primary Sunday school class.

Plan by the Mission

The disciple-making mission that the church adopts should influence conversation and the church calendar. Develop concrete plans that grow out of a unified sense of what God is calling the church to do. You will achieve increased clarity when the church is executing the mission, and this cannot happen unless the church is making plans based on its mission. Beholding the precision of the mission reflected in the activities of the church is a powerful way for others to come to understand and embrace the mission personally.

Decide What to Do. Planning the mission should identify and prioritize what activities will best reflect it. Beyond simple involvement, a disciple-making mission will influence *how* a church undertakes activities under the umbrella of the broader mission. The mission itself should shape each church activity, and viewing each activity through the lens of making disciples will adjust how the church approaches each activity. When making disciples is the ultimate destination, volunteers will view their roles in the common light of that emphasis.

Mission focus starts at the top. Taking a proactive approach with leadership staff allows planning to happen with the end in mind rather than reacting to opportunities as they arise. Planning is a thought-out strategy to make disciples; reacting leaves the leaders off balance and can lead to decisions secondary to the mission. Planning enables the leadership staff to develop unity as together they consider what should be implemented for the church to better make disciples. That question can be refined to suit a particular ministry, or addressed quarterly for additional emphasis, or tied closely to a specific event in church life; that is, flexibility in implementation may be useful. The act of planning bolsters a mission mindset among those involved in ministry.

Decide What Not to Do. Your leadership team may decide to suspend some church activities when they examine them with newfound mission clarity. If a program or activity does not effectively make disciples, it may need to stop. In many cases, this decision becomes resource driven rather than driven by thoroughly grasping the ministry's effectiveness for Christ. Accordingly, determining in advance that a ministry opportunity is not in the best interest of the church can save a church significant heartache.

Jesus gives advice about considering new endeavors and counting the cost of undertaking them before beginning: "For which of you, desiring to build a tower, does not first sit down and count the cost, whether he has enough to complete it? Otherwise, when he has laid a foundation and is not able to finish, all who see it begin to mock him, saying, 'This man began to build and was not able to finish'" (Luke 14:28–30). Jesus used this scenario to illustrate the sacrifice required to be Christ's disciples. Following Jesus, walking in His footsteps, and making more disciples comes at a cost. This cost is realized individually and corporately. Sometimes churches find themselves biting off more than they can chew, wondering why they became like the man whose building project exceeded his means to complete it.

Remember, God does not call a church to do everything. He calls us to examine our resources to focus on a few particular ministry endeavors. Sound stewardship will free churches from entanglements that sap their energy and deplete their resources. When the right opportunity comes along, a church stretched too thin may not be able to spare anyone to lead it. Eliminating mediocre opportunities enables the church to be ready for the fruitful ones.

When church members are recruited and mobilized according to their commitment to make disciples, there exists an opportunity for increased unity. A team centered on a mission that is clearly understood moves together in unity. Making disciples is the marching order of the believer, and churches function best when they recruit people already marching toward that objective.

Questions to Consider

1. Why are clarity and unity vital to preserving a church's mission?

2. How is unity of mission ensured among those who serve?

3. Who might be overlooked as a strong asset to help your church's mission?

4. What can your church do to identify the right people whose hearts are devoted to disciple-making?

5. What does your church do to maintain its mission clarity among staff?

CHAPTER 7

EVALUATE BY THE MISSION

Moving Targets

Harvest time had always been a joyous time for the farmers. Many expressed thankfulness for whatever their plants yielded. Some remembered the old days when harvest yielded thirty, sixty, or even a hundred times what they had planted, but those days were long passed. Despite the farmers' positive changes, they were still not producing as much as they had in days gone by. A double yield would be remarkable now. But overall, harvest time was happy and positive, an opportunity to share stories of the growing season and to celebrate success.

According to their custom, each farmer reported his results. All the farms in the area maintained this practice. Some did so annually, while others provided quarterly updates. Some even produced newsletters or made fancy graphs to highlight the most intriguing aspects of the growing season. Farmer and plant alike enjoyed these updates, which made them feel good about what was happening on the farm. The news of harvest made up for the reports from the farmer in charge of finances, who seemingly always denied purchases of much needed equipment.

The farmer who worked with seedlings was the first to report. There was nothing quite so endearing as seeing the little sprouts enjoy the newness of life in the sun! These young, tender plants needed nurture to give them the best start possible. Some of the plants recalled their own time in the plant nursery—a time when the nursery was packed with young plants! This was before the farmers had converted many of the seedling tables into equipment storage racks. Occasionally, someone would ask how the nursery could still be at capacity, but there was always an explanation as to why the farm should simply care for the plants they already had instead of adding more. This enlightenment usually involved a subtle admonishment about remaining thankful for the growth that was happening.

The farmer who worked mostly with the juvenile plants was known for his unique reports—and attire. Dressed in flip flops and a T-shirt rather than the traditional boots and overalls, he was a bemusing sight for others, who assumed he would adjust his wardrobe about the same time he shaved his neck scruff. This farmer took a long sip of his sixty-four-ounce convenience-store frozen drink and passionately explained his discovery of wild berry bushes in the woods. He spent much of his time foraging for the delicious berries! Any spoiled berries were put to good use as fertilizer for the plants, which was great for crop health. This, the others knew, was true, though they wondered if foraging was the best use of his time. His main task was to prune the growth on younger plants, so their energies would produce a good yield. No one voiced any concerns. The berries he brought and passed around were delicious, and people did not want to spoil the celebratory mood with unnecessary questions.

Each harvest update was similar. A farmer would explain what had happened throughout the season, and people would celebrate the results. Few asked if those results matched relevant goals or expectations. One farmer spent most of his time celebrating the yield of a crop that he had not planted. While his own plants fared poorly, some seed had blown from another area on the farm, and it was those plants he spent most of his time tending.

Although everyone celebrated the updates, they were unsure how those results matched expectations. No one wanted to spoil the positive atmosphere, but many quietly wondered how the positive reports related to the sense of defeat that many on the farm privately felt. Yields were lower, and resources were scarcer.

Principle #7: A church must maintain mission focus to stay effective at every level.

Success and Failure Belong to God

We must begin this section with a word of caution about evaluating disciple-making efforts. In both the personal call to believers and the specific mission of a local church, the measurement of the mission cannot simply be based on external outcomes. Christianity is littered with people whose heartfelt devotion was met with crushing defeat—if success is measured in raw numbers only. For example, missionaries have labored for decades with people who barely responded to the gospel.

Churches have poured countless resources into programs to make disciples, yet the visible fruit has been sparse. At the same time, some faithful churches have enjoyed numerical growth.

Other churches have taken theological shortcuts by watering down the message—and their programs may have attracted a crowd. The truth is, some churches with weak doctrine have become people magnets, but their fruit will not last. Many successful-looking churches have grown but at great theological expense. Their external growth does not correspond to internal spiritual growth among their members. To truth: external metrics of church success are an incomplete measure.

Ministry success cannot be measured using the same metrics we use to measure business success. Success or failure in God's eyes equates to faithfulness rather than observable results. It is always God who brings the results. Paul writes, "I planted, Apollos watered, but God gave the growth" (1 Cor. 3:6). The pursuit and evaluation of a ministry's success must take these truths into account.

When evaluating spiritual outcomes, some people shy away from evaluating in an objectively measurable way. But we should not be afraid to observe the observable: attendance grows, salvation decisions increase, parking becomes difficult, excitement buzzes, baptisms occur more often, and so on. As a result, momentum builds. Churches operating on mission often experience growth, and the visible growth points to supernatural activity—and can be measured by objective indicators in their midst.

Steward Your Talents

We know that God is the source of growth, yet He calls leaders to steward the ministries He has entrusted to them. Part of stewarding well involves planning for growth. The Parable of the Talents,[29] so often applied at the individual level, must also be applied at the leadership level. Servants were left in charge of resources. They understood that upon the master's return, He would call them to account. Just as the master's return was sudden, so the return of Christ will be. In the parable, the master expected an increase. Through the Great Commission, we understand Christ's expectation is an increase of disciples in His Kingdom.

The Lord will evaluate church leaders based on how effectively they made disciples. No one wants to mutter to the master, "Here, you have what is yours. I failed to make it increase." The unfaithful steward did not do anything unethical; he did not steal the money, borrow against it, or misappropriate it as some sort of business expense. He simply buried it. He gave the amount back in full. But his condemnation is hearing the master fire him with the words, "wicked and slothful servant" (Matt. 25:26).

How will the Master describe church leaders when He returns? How will He describe *you*?

The slothful are different from those who are lazy. Sloth exceeds laziness; its followers shrink from their duty out of timidity. Their actions in ministry efforts reveal that they are placing their confidence in human means rather than in a heavenly movement fueled by God's power. Christians do better to reflect on just how powerful God has been in the past—and rely on the Lord to work in *their* situations. The power of God is what enabled Israel to walk between two walls of water as they escaped the Egyptian hoard. It closed the jaws of the lions circling Daniel all night. It kept Peter's feet on the water's surface when he stepped out of the boat.

If we look more closely, we see that Peter experienced both the breathtaking power of God and the spectacular failure of man that night. After a few divinely empowered steps, Peter's timidity emerged, grew, and conquered within seconds. Faced with the buffeting winds, the stinging rain, and the surging waves, a few square inches of supernatural surface tension were not enough in Peter's estimation to keep him moving toward Christ. Peter sank due to fear, believing he must focus on the surrounding storm rather than on Christ.

The Apostle Paul understood the power of timidity that tempts us to shrink from duty. He used the same term for *slothfulness* when he wrote this to the Roman believers: "Do not be slothful in zeal, be fervent in spirit, serve the Lord" (Rom. 12:11).[30] Sloth can be a wet blanket to a Christian's zeal, while a fervent spirit throws off the wet blanket and serves the Lord. The fervent spirit prevails when a person understands God's power—the same power that parted the Red Sea and closed the lions' mouths. A fervent spirit knows God's power is at work in our efforts to make disciples. To those same Roman believers, Paul wrote, "For I am not ashamed of the gospel, for it is the power of God for salvation to everyone who believes" (Rom. 1:16). Believers who experience the most vibrant Christian life both affirm the power of the gospel unto salvation and step into ministry expecting to be led by their powerful Lord.

As He did with the Romans, Paul reminded Timothy not to shrink back from his duty: "For God gave us a spirit not of fear but of power and love and self-control. Therefore do not be ashamed of the testimony about our Lord, nor of me his prisoner, but share in suffering for the gospel by the power of God" (2 Tim. 1:7–8). Lest anyone think stepping out in confidence in God is a technique to manufacture one's own destiny—a parlor trick for ministry success—Paul explains that stepping out courageously for the cause of the gospel is likely to involve suffering. When Peter was walking on water, the storm that swirled around him was real. It was emblematic of the trials believers would face when they strive to make disciples.

Evaluating by the mission assumes God's power is at work, urging His people to step out in their efforts to further His Kingdom. Many church leaders, however, are guilty of holding a maintenance mindset rather than a multiplication mindset. Maintenance requires effort to account for their hours of labor among God's people as they keep their ministry ship afloat.

But God does not call church leaders merely to keep the ship afloat. He calls them to build a fleet. To use one of Jesus's metaphors, elders are not called simply to watch over the flock; they are called to shepherd it, bringing an increase of health and vitality.[31] Too many church leaders expect too little, equating faithfulness with maintaining the status quo. Although your flock may not be transformed right away—and you may face hardship or criticism—God has called you to be strategic as you consider how to expand the investment God has entrusted to you. Doing the work of an evangelist as you live as an example to the flock is part of fulfilling your ministry.[32]

Does your church have one hundred people? What discipleship activities are you deploying to sow gospel seed to increase your harvest twofold? Should you consider planting a church so that there are two growing congregations? Who among the church can be nurtured for ministry leadership? Where can your church partner with other churches to better shower the community with God's love? Good stewardship requires leaders to teach their people to scatter seed.

So, how does a church leader evaluate his church's efforts? In *The Vine Project*, Colin Marshall and Tony Payne explain,

> If we're going to make any significant progress in bringing real and lasting change and improvement to our church or ministry, we need to arrive at a clear, honest picture of where we're starting from. We need to understand where our convictions are being lived, practiced, and expressed, and where they are not. We need to understand where the real problems are, as well as where the real potential is. Without honestly and openly confronting the facts of our situation, any plans or desires about changing the culture or making progress in disciple-making are just wishful thinking. This honest evaluation has an important side benefit. It helps to build a sense of urgency; it makes it painfully clear to us that things cannot stay as they are.[33]

The term *evaluation* often evokes a defensive response, but, when done correctly, evaluation helps sharpen the mission-oriented church, keeping it an effective tool for Christ. Without evaluation, people tend to drift, developing their own ministry targets.

Mission-Oriented Evaluation

What does evaluation according to the mission entail? It begins when a church considers how well its resources and activities are leveraged toward making disciples. This is more than simply considering whether existing programs are geared toward discipleship. It involves evaluating and developing the right attitude within her members. Are you teaching them to think like the faithful stewards who multiplied the talents—or like the servant who buried it? Evaluation needs parameters and must occur at the visionary, structural, and program levels.

Visionary Evaluation

God has given church leaders the tasks of casting vision for a God-ordained discipleship emphasis, then mapping how to achieve it strategically. This responsibility involves developing the mission, the mindset, and the methods described in chapter 5, along with planning resourcefully and creatively to accomplish that mission in the best way. The evaluation of leadership includes asking leaders some probing questions:

- To what extent is the vision of our church derived from God through prayer, studying Scripture, and God's call for our church as considered by our leadership team?

- What evidence suggests a fervent spirit in the Lord toward this mission? What evidence suggests we are slothful, not zealous?

- How have circumstances in the past six months propelled us toward the mission or curtailed our progress?

- Where have our efforts skewed away from the mission, even by a small degree?

- Who among us articulates the same mission described by the leaders?

Structural Evaluation

A church or ministry's structure is about people. Structure comprises the organizational parameters and pathways that enable people to flourish within the organization. Colin

Marshall and Tony Payne made this point in their book *The Trellis and the Vine*, illustrating that churches with the right trellis structure enable the growth of the vine. They explain:

> Trellis work . . . often looks more impressive than vine work. It's more visible and structural. We can point to something tangible—a committee, an event, a program, a budget, an infrastructure—and say that we have achieved something. We can build our trellis till it reaches to the heavens, in the hope of making a name for ourselves, but there may still be very little growth in the vine. [34]

Patterns of growth develop from church ministry structures, which shape the culture and outlook of the people. Churches create systems for how things get done and who does them. Pastor Robby Gallaty has often remarked, "Your system is perfectly designed to give you the results you're getting."[35] Similarly, management consultant W. Edwards Deming observes, "A bad system will beat a good person every time."[36] We have all experienced this phenomenon. We know the frustration of calling a customer support line only to be transferred from department to department. A seemingly simple issue becomes a chain of transferred calls that eats up forty-five minutes and provides little resolution.

We can learn from that frustration. Do the structural systems in your church enhance or inhibit spiritual growth? Do they encourage or hinder ministry involvement? Are they clear and understandable?

Some churches operate with a system that is known only to a select few members who have been serving for years. Newer members find it difficult to become part of the "in" group who know how the system works. Because this structure is built upon subjective principles, only a certain type of member has access to the inner workings. This forfeits valuable perspectives from outside the system. The blind spots created by this absence of counsel decreases ministry impact.

Other churches attempt to create structures that enable growth but find themselves contending with an invisible layer that inhibits effectiveness. We might say that a power behind the power exists, and an unofficial authority in the church seems to hold all the keys. People do not flourish in a system that has an unspoken "church boss" because church bosses may hold others hostage and prevent ministry effectiveness.

Another type of tussle appears if church leaders fail to develop a coherent structure of systems, leaving people unsure how to get involved beyond the most apparent ministry needs. Creativity is stifled in these settings, as few discover clear structural support for ministry growth.

In contrast, a well-defined structure will safeguard the people, experienced or new, while supporting and encouraging their growth and creative ministry involvement. This structure necessarily flows from a vision that motivates people to grow in ministry. It also empowers them to carry it out.

The safeguarding aspect of structure is based in theology. Several New Testament passages warn church leaders to protect the doctrine of the church. Regarding the pastor's role, "He must hold firm to the trustworthy word as taught, so that he may be able to give instruction in sound doctrine and also to rebuke those who contradict it" (Titus 1:9).[37] Only on the foundation of doctrine can leaders build the necessary structural walls. Further, the pastor must ensure the right leaders, both paid and volunteers, are in the right positions on those walls.

A Special Consideration. Jesus elevated the importance of children when He said, "Whoever causes one of these little ones who believe in me to sin, it would be better for him if a great millstone were hung around his neck and he were thrown into the sea" (Mark 9:42). Protecting children in the church is critical! Recent history has taught churches the importance of screening and training volunteers for their children's ministry. Dropping the ball on qualifying workers can yield devastating results that hurt the child and ravage a ministry. Wise leaders will be vigilant to instill boundaries and hold regular training to ensure their children's program is above suspicion.

Safeguarding children is vital, just as helping them grow in Christ is vital. Churches must develop a child protection policy that keeps children safe while also allowing the children's ministry to function smoothly. A policy that puts an enormous burden on volunteers will reduce the number of volunteers. Nonetheless, a church must find a structure that finds the sweet spot between compliance and mobilization so that an optimal balance is achieved.[38]

Program Evaluation

Ministry programs are a lot like children. They are a bit messy, require a lot of feeding, and each person in the church has a few they find special. Parents understand the daily struggle to ensure meals are ready, laundry is clean, and homework is completed. They know the challenge to attend the soccer game across town, shuttle their kids to piano lessons, and manage their own work responsibilities. Oh, and we cannot forget the school play and the need to buy a new pair of pants because of a child's sudden growth spurt. Ministry programs can feel a lot like that!

Leaders are always managing a list of passages to study, people to contact, materials to send, and resources to investigate—while the deadlines of the next lesson or planning meeting loom. For many leaders, we would not have it any other way. The members and visitors to our churches are worth it. Nonetheless, honest evaluation should lead to increased effectiveness, making all those efforts *even more* worth it. Aubrey Malphurs admonishes, "Every leader should ask, 'Am I evaluating my ministry effectiveness, and do we evaluate the effectiveness of the church?' If the church's mission is to make disciples, the evaluative request of the senior pastor is, 'Show me our disciples!'"[39] The importance of program-level evaluation cannot be overstated.

For many, the program is where the theoretical and abstract become concrete. People are more likely to embrace what they can see, hear, and touch. Perhaps that is why John begins his first epistle, "That which was from the beginning, which we have heard, which we have seen with our eyes, which we looked upon and have touched with our hands, concerning the word of life . . ." (1 John 1:1). Because the apostles had physically experienced Jesus, they better proclaimed His message so that others could experience Jesus and spread His message too.

God does not need church programs for His people to carry out the Great Commission. Faith in Christ and obedience to the Lord's commands are all that are needed for that. But church programs have become a primary method for people to carry out the mission of the church. Because a church program is the primary means to proclaim the gospel, people who are involved can use their experience and apply it to their interactions with others. People better understand how to live out their faith through church ministry programs like small group Bible studies, outreaches to children, a sports ministry, greeting and following up with guests, and so on. Faith finds tangible expression through programs.

Ways to Evaluate Programs

Several churches have ministries that, although good, need improvement. Developing a process of evaluation helps improve alignment with the church's discipleship mission. Such alignment-oriented evaluation "is critical to the organization," explains Aubrey Malphurs. "Accomplishing alignment bridges the gap, preserving the ministry's core values, reinforcing its vision, and catalyzing constant movement toward the mission."[40] Just as churches experience mission drift, so do programs. It makes logical sense: programs are smaller than the overall church, so mission drift occurs at the program level before it infects the church as a whole. Evaluating programs to keep them on mission benefits the church in two ways: 1) It keeps the program on target; 2) One level higher, it also keeps the church focused on the bull's-eye. Programs are the "how" of the church's mission. The two go hand in hand.

To Begin or Not to Begin. The first step in program evaluation addresses whether to start it in the first place. Ministry leaders should do a little family planning. A program will require resources: people, space, money, and communication, each of them limited. The people in a church have a finite number of hours available. The church building has a limited number of rooms. Leaders must also keep an eye on funding when contemplating launching a program. Less obvious, a church has limited communication opportunities: more programs lead to more requests for announcements, which may crowd others out. When you step back and assess the decision factors for starting a new program, you realize how important it is to make the decision carefully. We should also remember that a program is not only an outreach to the community but also tangible expressions of Christ's love for God's glory. Therefore, the evaluation process and resulting decision should be executed with an excellence that pleases the Lord and shows God's heart for the world.

The leadership of the church should launch any new program, and it should have a purpose and mission that point directly to Scripture. The mission statement will form the nucleus of future evaluation. For instance, if a program's mission involves serving low-income residents in the area, an evaluation might address why most of the impacted people are well-off. The right leadership and resources should be in place, and the church should be told why the ministry is starting. This encourages people to pray and be involved.

Considerations Regarding Starting Permanent Programs. It may be best to begin a program as a temporary pilot, making it permanent if it shows considerable promise. Some of today's thriving ministry opportunities began as a summer project or short-term study. Similarly, pursue a tournament rather than a league, or a one-year commitment to a quarterly outreach rather than an enduring effort every week. These short-term opportunities, offered on a rotating basis, may prevent burnout among your volunteers. The objective is to determine which, if any, short-term programs should be granted long-term status. Planning by mission principles helps leaders work through all associated ministry and program decisions.

We should think of it like this: unleash your people to serve on their own. The small group Bible study is a compact Great Commission engine. When you encourage members to volunteer in ministry, the people who have already been serving in these groups may be the very ones who organize activities on their own. What a great situation: God has called all Christians to serve others in Jesus's name, and self-starters step up to the plate before the church establishes a program to do so. Structured programs inside the church provide a healthy added layer of oversight. Nevertheless, the healthiest option for many ministry opportunities is simply to encourage people to go for it in Jesus's name. Many people find that working in a small group affords a good bonding between members and attracts others who see the hands and feet of Jesus in action.

Evaluation Considerations. Church leaders are wise to evaluate programs periodically. (This is different from the visionary evaluation that happens before a program is launched.) Such evaluation can help reveal what is and is not working. Understanding what is working requires a firm grasp on the mission of the church. Consider the following questions when evaluating a program:

- How is this program accomplishing its stated purpose or mission?

- In what ways does this program help people grasp the tangible expression of their faith?

- How is this program accomplishing the church's disciple-making mission?

- Were there any stated objectives? If so, which ones were met?

- If we failed to meet any objectives, what prevented success?

- What adjustments might help this program better accomplish its mission and the church's mission?

When evaluating, give praise! No program will be perfectly efficient, and most will involve volunteers. In all cases, God takes our feeble efforts and uses them for His glory. Give thanks to God for what He has done through the program. Then, as good stewards, consider what we can do to make it more effective.

Track What Matters. People maintain records of what matters to them. Evaluation should include metrics to help ascertain a ministry's effectiveness. What is the attendance growth rate compared to prior years? How many pounds of food did we distribute this season compared to last? How many people took measurable steps of faith because of this ministry?

One of the most effective ways to gauge results is by measuring deeper faith commitments that people may make. Eric Geiger and Thom Rainer make this point in their book *Simple Church,* stating, "Your church's ability to get people to take their next steps will determine the level of success you will have in creating transformational environments."[41] Find ways to help programs encourage people to increase their Christian expression—to grow in Christ—then track the progress. Your approach should not put people in a box but rather allow the church to measure and evaluate its own ministry effectiveness.

Ending a Program. Ministries are sometimes like government agencies: once started, they are almost impossible to stop. Churches continue to support them because they have already supported them. When it comes time to terminate a program, some attached members can be offended or hurt; leaders should not be surprised by this and work to mitigate it through extensive communication, personal counsel, and so on.

It is of course OK that programs do not last forever. They serve their time for a season until they no longer meet the objectives they set out to accomplish. There are many reasons for this, including changes to the community's needs, changes in the church, updated technology—or by meeting all the objectives! There may even be widespread interest in moving to a new opportunity.

Toward the end of a ministry's lifespan, there may not be a need to put it out to pasture: a few resolute people may still wish to be involved, and that can also be OK. They can still serve Christ through that ministry, even though their impact may be limited. Whether it ends abruptly or gradually, remember that dedicated people are invested; be sure to demonstrate how much you value them even as a beloved program is phased out.

Rely upon God

We must remember that God does not need our programs, nor does He need our great ideas, capable efforts, or wise management. He calls us to serve Him faithfully, doing our best to steward that which He has entrusted to us. A poorly organized church whose people hit their knees regularly to petition and thank God is far better off than a well-run congregation with well-ordered structures and slick communication—but little or no prayer. Although being a good steward is something God asks, He has never once depended on your competence. Often, however, He has performed wondrously through your weakness.

The most important evaluation question is, "Are we depending on God and seeking His face?"

Questions to Consider

1. Why should those pursuing the evaluation process acknowledge that God is ultimately sovereign over our efforts?

2. What does your church do to evaluate the effectiveness of its vision, structure, and ministries?

3. How do numerical and spiritual growth indicate the success of a program? How might they not tell the full picture?

4. What can your church do to improve the way it evaluates its efforts?

CHAPTER 8

ALLOCATE FOR THE MISSION

Timely Cooperation

Life in the field was rewarding but often draining too. Chores had to be done, fields needed tending, plants required staking, fences demanded mending, and tractor repairs were all too common. Added concerns came with the heavy workload. Wind blew off row covers, pests threatened crop health, and an excess of sun or rain threatened to negate the painstaking efforts. The tired farmers found themselves prone to griping about their concerns.

Some believed too much attention was being given to greenhouse work and ant activities. "If those folks came and helped us," they argued, "we would be able to get all our work done." But the greenhouse and ant farmers felt just as overworked as the others, and now they felt less appreciated. "Our farm has a good reputation in the area because of what we do!" countered the ant farmers. "And we are known," added the greenhouse farmers, "for our specialized care for each individual plant." How could the farm cease these essential functions just to help what the farmers in the field were doing?

With no resolution in sight, tensions remained at a simmer—until things got worse. The farmer in charge of finances explained that a new tractor could not be purchased this year. As disappointing as this news was, even more shocking was the news that the farm could not continue to pay the farmers much longer. The farmers were understandably concerned: Should they sell some of their land? Would they need to let a few farmers go? Was there hope that this year's crop production would be better?

For a short while, the bickering among the farmers continued. The field farmers said the lack of help transitioning back to outdoor farming was the problem. The ant farmers declared the ant activities were the system that kept the farm going. The greenhouse farmers stated their potting approach kept the plants the happiest and that happy plants produce more.

The conflict appeared ready to boil over, and indeed would have, were it not for the efforts of one of the farmers' wives. This woman, a farmer in her own right, had been frequently spotted looking over the farm from the hillside: the fields, the greenhouses, the ant activity centers—all of it. She was no stranger to the various farm areas either. Everyone could expect to receive a smile from her, and all knew that she loved the farm.

Though she was eloquent, she preferred interaction to speeches. First, she brought one of the greenhouse farmers over to the ant facility. Accompanied by one of the ant farmers, she explained that some new plants had come for the ant activities but that they needed tending. The greenhouse farmer had not seen new plants to care for in some time and readily agreed to treat them. The ant farmer was later excited to learn how well the new plants were doing. Along with some other plants, these now-healthy plants were ready for the outdoors.

Again, the farmer's wife connected with the farmers, this time with one of the field farmers. Together with the greenhouse farmer, they found the perfect place to transplant the rehabilitated plants. The field farmer even followed the greenhouse farmer's advice to put a fabric screen above the plants for a couple of weeks to protect them. Later, the greenhouse farmer was elated upon hearing the plants were producing and that some of their seed would be harvested for the next planting.

Then, the field and ant farmers, encouraged by the recent progress, developed a planting plan together. Instead of holding events in the ant facility, they experimented with bringing the ants out to a field just before planting time to hold events there. This allowed the soil to be worked while highlighting the beauty and health of the other crops. The ants were then involved in working the soil of the field as the farmers scattered the seed collected from the prior harvest.

Through the influence of the farmer's wife, the farmers altered their practices just a bit to improve their progress and success. They also began to understand better how their work related to the other farmers and to the overall success of the farm.

The financial situation on the farm began to change too, as the farmers collaborated to leverage their efforts not to meet individual responsibilities but for the farm itself.

The farmer in charge of finances reported that the fancy new tractor could finally be purchased! By then, however, there was less need for a tractor and more need for space. The farmers considered acquiring more farmland to expand their fields so they could scatter more seed.

The workload had not changed, but the farmers had been changed by it. By laboring together, they now viewed needs collectively rather than individually, and they collaborated to find solutions. The ants had changed, too. Their once-separate activities were now more directly tied to plant health and to working the soil to receive seed. The plants became increasingly focused on seed production rather than on external features. Extraneous growth was often pruned to better facilitate fruiting. Thus, the farm had plenty of harvest to share with the community.

The farm was beginning again to see the bountiful returns described by the Master Gardener.

Principle #8: The mission succeeds when people cooperatively contribute to its success.

Mission-Centered Stewardship

God has unlimited resources. He who formed the earth—carving out its seas, shaping its mountains, and lavishing the land with goodness—is a God of abundance. Those who would seek to accomplish God's mission can do so because the power of an infinite God is at work through them. The Apostle Paul wrote of his own labors for the mission, stating, "For this I toil, struggling with all his energy that he powerfully works within me" (Col. 1:29). Christians who faithfully pursue the Great Commission can adopt a mindset of abundance, not scarcity!

Yet this same infinite God somehow encapsulated Himself in human flesh and became intimately familiar with human limitations. Jesus knew hunger, fatigue, pain, and poverty. Unlike foxes and birds who had places to live, the Son of Man frequently had no place to rest.[42] But the meager circumstances did not stop Jesus; He never seemed to operate from the perspective of scarcity. More than once He took a paltry lunch and multiplied it to feed a multitude. The lean becomes lavish in God's economy. Conversely, resources normally associated with wealth were used for everyday purposes. The apparent scandal of expensive perfume used to wash the feet of Jesus reminds us that our valuations differ from God's. Whether through plentiful or penniless circumstances, God's mission can expand.

The mission is not dependent upon the means allocated to accomplish it. Instead, it is dependent upon the God whose power is at work through people who are willing conduits. Ten dollars with God's power is far greater than a thousand dollars without it. Mission-centered stewardship is primarily an affirmation of faith in the mission Giver. Whatever He has entrusted into your care to accomplish the mission can be either multiplied or concentrated toward His good purpose. God has given your church all the resources it needs to accomplish its mission.

From an asset perspective, your church has been equipped by God for the ministry it has been called to accomplish. The children's director knows how many people are needed in the nursery this Sunday. The secretary knows how many bulletins to print each week. The building manager knows how many chairs to set up in each Sunday school room. Expectations born from experience have already framed much of the planning for the church's ministry.

But the numbers behind our preplanning may reveal something about our restrained subconscious expectations. Why are more chairs not set up? Why are more bulletins not printed? Perhaps our expectations reveal our lack of commitment to making disciples.

Peter and John were walking to the temple for what was likely becoming a routine: proclaiming the good news of Jesus to the people. Then they met a lame beggar who, by God's power, was about to be dramatically healed. Suddenly a huge crowd formed, eager to witness the healing and to discover the power behind it.

Did the apostles expect this miraculous work of God to take place in their midst? Had they traveled to the temple with a sense of expectation that the God of plenty would work mightily among them? In terms we understand, had they printed enough bulletins? If you listen carefully to what Peter said, you may see that the apostles walked in confidence of God's abundant blessing. They exuded expectant readiness.

Peter's response reveals it all: "I have no silver and gold, but what I do have I give to you. In the name of Jesus Christ of Nazareth, rise up and walk!" (Acts 3:6). Peter's wallet was empty. His tangible resources were scarce. But Peter's attitude reflected, "No silver? No gold? No problem!" Maybe he recalled David's words to the giant Goliath: "You come to me with a sword and with a spear and with a javelin, but I come to you in the name of the LORD of hosts" (1 Sam. 17:45). God's mission carried out with God's power is the calling of God's people.

When fulfilling our disciple-making mission, external resources are a bonus. The greatest resource is the calling of God that lands on a willing heart. Orient your heart toward the God whose power is at work in you. Then accomplish wonders.

Resource Allocation

God tends to add additional resources to our willing hearts. He will give us resources to make disciples, and responsible stewardship involves using those resources for His glory. A church has four primary resources: time, money, people, and space. Our job is to steward those resources, directing them toward making disciples.

By definition, allocation implies separation. From the whole, a portion is separated (allocated) for a particular purpose. These resources, from a physical perspective, are indeed finite. At any given time, a church has a certain number of members, chairs, choir robes, classrooms, dollars, and sleeves of disposable coffee cups. The church must decide how to allocate each of them.

Allocate Time

All churches are on equal footing regarding available time. Each member is allocated twenty-four hours a day. How that time is used is another matter. At the church level, the events and programs on the church calendar represent the priorities of the church. Because time is a limited commodity, mission effectiveness requires the wise prioritization of our calendars. Many churches become bound by calendar clutter, finding that program commitments prevent allocating time to new endeavors. By reevaluating the calendar, a church can ensure it is prioritizing activities geared toward making disciples.

When churches shut down their ministries in the spring of 2020, many had the opportunity to reevaluate their calendar priorities. Some churches, having experienced the struggles of overcommitment, were newly intentional about returning events to the calendar when restrictions were lifted. A similar calendar shutdown is unlikely, yet it is certainly possible to evaluate your church's use of time. Finding ways to organize the calendar around their objectives reveals its mission faithfulness.

Church leadership must consider the value of the meaning of Sabbath and other life rhythms when designing the church calendar. We should reflect on how much more Israel could have accomplished for the Lord without a "wasted" day of rest! Or should we? We must not forget that God is not only looking for His children to be productive; He wants our hearts to be drawn to Him as we enjoy the world He created. Although He called us to make disciples, He also called us to rest and appreciate His goodness. This practice, designed for our good, can help us become more effective at making disciples!

The call to rest on the Sabbath reveals what God knows about how He designed us: our productivity wanes when we push too hard. *New York Times* author Tony Schwartz explains,

> More and more of us find ourselves unable to juggle overwhelming demands and maintain a seemingly unsustainable pace. Paradoxically, the best way to get more done may be to spend more time doing less. A new and growing body of multidisciplinary research shows that strategic renewal ... boosts productivity, job performance, and of course, health.

Schwartz adds, "The importance of restoration is rooted in our physiology. Human beings aren't designed to expend energy continuously."[43] Christians should already be familiar with the need for rest. Jesus, our Great Commissioner, explains that His goal is for us to find rest as we follow Him. We would do well to soak in His words: "Come to me, all who labor and are heavy laden, and I will give you rest. Take my yoke upon you, and learn from me, for I am gentle and lowly in heart, and you will find rest for your souls. For my yoke is easy, and my burden is light" (Matt. 11:28–30).

Rest facilitates our trust in the God who empowers the mission. Eric Geiger and Kevin Peck exclaim, "In an age where employers are known for using and leveraging 'human resources,' what a wondrous reality that the God of the universe does not leverage us, but instead has designed us to be objects of His mercy and grace."[44] God wants His people to enjoy Him foremost and, rather than rely on our own strength, petition Him to be at work for His glory. Prioritizing the mission involves relying on the God who empowers it. An hour spent in prayer about the mission is worth ten hours fulfilling it in our own strength. We should celebrate and petition our Lord as we set aside time to make disciples in His name.

Allocate Money

Just as people wisely create financial plans to pursue their goals, God calls churches to direct financial resources toward what is most important. Kennon Callahan underscores how important monetary decisions are for a church when he writes, "Congregations who practice effective church finances have a stronger mission, help more people, and raise more money. Their mission is increased."[45] Churches that are serious about making disciples ensure that adequate funds are directed toward that purpose.

Allocating money toward the mission comes down to stewardship. God will call His servants to account for how they used their money. Whether funds are bountiful or scarce, consider how they must be directed toward the mission God has called your church to fulfill. This may include prioritizing the programs in which disciples are being reached and taught most effectively. Consider the scriptural principle that the one who is faithful with little will be entrusted with much.[46]

Leaders should also keep in mind that cash flow is downstream of the mission. People will be motivated to give if the mission is to make disciples, and the more they understand what they are funding, the greater their sense of purpose in giving. "Raising finances is a visionary measure," explains Aubrey Malphurs. "People's giving response will often tell you something about the quality of your church's vision and the leader's ability to cast that vision."[47] Giving often reflects the unity of a church around its mission.

Allocate People

The idea of allocating people may invoke a negative, impersonal connotation. The church, however, is composed of the people of God, and they are its greatest resource. Allocation in this sense involves creating roles and pathways to help people find their ministry niche as they make disciples. People are the indispensable element to mission success; they are the keystone to optimal mission allocation. The church that funds events and allocates space for them will regularly succeed only when the right people are put in place as well. Reaching people is the goal, and the primary means of reaching people is through other people.

The incarnation of Christ portrays the criticality of sending a person to carry out a mission. The Father did not send a message, speak from heaven, or use a literal lamb to redeem His people. He sent His Son, who accomplished all that the Father had sent Him to do. Jesus understood the Father's plan to redeem people, and He played His part to accomplish it.

Walking in the footsteps of Christ, Christians are to understand the role of the church in redeeming people and helping them grow as new believers as they play their part in the execution of that mission. "We are Christians," write Eric Geiger and Kevin Peck, "because others have shared the gospel with us. We have matured because others have helped develop us."[48] Help people make the best—and usually shortest—possible connection between their efforts and accomplishing the mission. Give them the most important reason to involve themselves in other people's lives.

Allocate Space

Space encompasses physical resources like a classroom or building. Bible studies need a place to meet, while an outreach may need a field, gym, or fellowship hall. But they also need other physical resources; if the church has a van, how can it be used toward the disciple-making mission? Wise leaders view the physical spaces of the church as resources to help make disciples: they understand God has entrusted that space to them. Alvin Lindgren encourages each church to "utilize all her resources . . . in the fulfillment of her mission."[49] God, in His masterful providence, went to great lengths to bring that space into existence and then leverage it for His glory. It is our job to do the same.

God's concern for properly using physical space and attendant items is evident throughout Scripture. Chapters are devoted to specific instructions for the construction of the tabernacle. Lists record the donations of various objects for temple purposes. The New Testament highlights the importance given to often mundane physical items: they are tools that can and should be used to His glory. The early church, for instance, shared their meager possessions according to the needs of fellow believers.[50]

Because God designed us to complete His mission for us in the physical world, the assets within the world are a means to give God glory as we seek to do His will. Because God is the source of all our resources, leveraging them well often yields being entrusted with more. Therefore, in prayerful consideration, do not be afraid to support the mission of disciple-making generously via physical improvements. Rooms can be renovated into more welcoming spaces, building projects can be initiated, and investments in digital tools can broadly expand reach. Math wizards are vital for the financial health of the church, yet, by His grace, the math may not always add up in God's ledger as it might in man's. Consider how certain assets can best be used for your mission, allocate generously, and ask God to provide for any differences.

Allocating the Intangibles

Churches sometimes face challenges that are less about resources and more about their mindset. All churches have some level of resources to carry out the disciple-making mission. Even if those resources are scarce, the One who multiplied loaves and fish specializes in stretching them for His glory. Oil jars remain full when they are used to accomplish the Lord's will.[51] In God's economy, shortages are miracles in waiting. A church that exhibits trust in God and commitment to the mission can step out in faith and begin allocating resources great or small for God's glory. The results may be miraculous.

Allocate Intentionally

Using entrusted resources wisely involves intentionality. Alan Raughton shares, "A church that is serious about reaching, teaching, and serving . . . knows the importance of providing appropriate space and resources to accomplish this work."[52] Churches can use their resources toward meeting their mission and not merely sustaining their structure. Sometimes a church falls victim to its own calendar: as mentioned earlier, so many events are scheduled that resources cannot easily be allocated to a new endeavor. For example, if the fellowship hall is reserved for a ladies' tea event, it cannot simultaneously host the youth dodgeball event.[53] Calendar complications require us to be creative as we maintain focus on the objectives the church seeks to accomplish. A mission-focused church must consider the means it will employ to carry out its Great Commission calling. Such consideration involves periodically taking stock of how resources are being used and how they might be otherwise directed.

In some churches, very little resource allocation occurs. An example might be the construction of the fellowship hall decades earlier—whatever the original intent for its use, that objective may now be irrelevant. Sometimes this happens during a leadership transition, or when members migrate elsewhere, or it simply happens over time, but a church can recover its God-given mission and reassess its use of resources in light of it. Restoring an intentional mission mindset for resource management helps align those resources with making disciples.

Resources are where the rubber meets the road to accomplish the mission. The mission is aspirational, but allocation makes it tangible. Just as a program is the most visible aspect of the mission, the allocation of resources exposes the reality of how a church is pursuing their identified mission. Because the church is composed of Christians, allocation for the mission impacts the people too, and they will hopefully see practical ways to set aside their portion of the resources astutely to grow the discipling culture of the church. Communication of the mission and the opportunity for individuals to support it create a positive snowball effect.

Allocate Creatively

Because your church enjoys a unique setting, you have unique opportunities to allocate to the mission. A church's history, location, people, reputation, and past partnerships are among the many factors that can spark imagination as you lead people to carry out God's disciple-making call. Finding creative ways to allocate goes beyond a standard form that may determine a budget amount, classroom space, or meeting night. It engages the minds of people, asking them to consider how God has prepared each of them to make disciples in their respective contexts.

One church in Texas determined that part of its mission was to develop a strong set of men's and women's Bible studies. Early in its growth phase, the church lacked both sufficient meeting space and childcare areas. Their creative solution was to alternate weeks: one week the men stayed home to care for the children while the women went to their study, and the next week they switched. Their attendance soared in short order. The church gave priority to announcing the schedule, and the women knew they had a night to enjoy the

Christian fellowship they craved. The men, who by nature are less likely to engage in such studies, found themselves within a construct that scheduled them to attend, where they were soon building solid relationships. That simple system became a catalyst for both spiritual and numerical growth.[54]

Obstacles are often opportunities viewed from a different angle. A church's greatest hurdles often present unique prospects for growth. The waters of the Red Sea presented an imposing obstacle to the Israelites, whose Egyptian pursuers had them pinned down. With God's intervention, that sea became the Egyptians' tomb, and God's people were found on the opposite shore, filled with praise at the awesome work of the Lord.[55] The challenges churches face can experience similar transformations when God's people trust Him.

Such trust requires creative faith and a listening ear for God's direction. The Israelites crossed a different body of water—the Jordan River—when entering the Promised Land. This time they were not escaping an enemy but confronting one.[56] They were on a mission. Unlike the Red Sea's parting, God required that Israel's leaders first step into the waters before He would miraculously stop them further upstream. God often calls leaders to step out in faith and trust that God will act on their behalf.

Allocate Cooperatively

The alignment of God's people toward making disciples is a powerful thing. When believers view each aspect of their ministry as cooperatively helping people know and grow in Christ, their activities soon burst with connection points that build unity and catalyze dynamic growth in the church. When such an environment exists—when the disciple-making mission has been woven into the fabric of the church community—the boundaries between ministries and programs begin to fade. The women's ministry makes disciples among ladies but is quick to make connections with their husbands, establishing a connection to men as well. The men are familiar with the children's ministry calendar and look to draw an acquaintance to the next children's outreach. Leaders in the children's ministry tell parents who are disconnected from Bible study about the new small group beginning soon. Small group members make connections with church softball teammates to help them step from the softball diamond into the sanctuary. As we can see, churches that cooperatively operate pursuant to a disciple-making mission find that their people allocate not only their energies but also their hearts and minds toward a singular goal.

Opportunity Allocation

Financial investors understand a key principle about resources related to the stock market: when an opportunity arrives, have funds ready to invest. When the market takes a downturn, they "buy the dip" for a stock expected to rebound. But if investment funds are tied up, they may then have to sell at a loss to buy that other stock. Wise investors understand they should keep some capital in reserve for just such an opportunity.

Churches should consider a similar practice. If they can steward their resources well, they will have some in reserve when opportunities arise. Consider operating within margins—perhaps at eight-five percent capacity—to allow for the unexpected mission opportunities that God may bring. Doing so is itself an act of faith, and it will put less strain on God's people as they carry out the mission to make disciples.

Questions to Consider

1. Why must a church's mission enjoy significant energy to succeed?

2. What budget allocations in your church indicate a concerted desire to reach and grow disciples?

3. How can people be motivated to give their time, money, and energy to your church's mission?

4. What special opportunities can your church leverage to further its mission?

5. How does allocation toward the mission develop unity within the church?

CHAPTER 9

MOTIVATE BY THE MISSION

As productivity hummed along on the farm, some farmers and plants were still slow to respond. Plants and people alike needed a wee bit of nurture and encouragement to keep them going. The old ways of encouraging them, however, seemed insufficient. The farmers had retained a few maxims from their less productive times to keep themselves motivated. They would say, for example, "Appease the plants; their beauty enhance." This line came from the not-too-distant days when individually potting plants was the standard practice. Because seed was purchased rather than produced, farmers believed the appearance of the plants was the best reflection of the plants' own happiness. Now the saying rang hollow for most of the farmers: were they not supposed to appease— or please—the Master Gardener rather than the plants? And did the Master Gardener not say that the result of their efforts would be bountiful harvests?

Another statement bandied about was, "Care for ants is care for plants." This motto, from the heady days of ant farming, was not necessarily wrong so much as it was misleading. When ant activities had become a goal in themselves, the ant farmers had become exclusively devoted to the six-legged creatures, becoming disconnected from plant growth altogether. While working with ants could lead to plant productivity, the circus-like productions arranged by the ants had been more about soil entertainment than plant health. Many of those ant activities were still organized, but the farmers worked with greater care to connect them more directly to plants, their root health, and ultimately, their fruit.

Plants, too, experienced changes in their nurture. Some still underwent pruning, though it was no longer for appearance but for their increased production. This was particularly true in the vineyard, which had received special instructions from the Master Gardener not long before he had left them. The standard for what constituted a healthy plant became clear: appearance and variation mattered far less than hardiness and yield.

New mottos began to take hold around the farm—sayings that reflected a recovery to garden the way the Master Gardener had shown them, such as, "Full fields bring high yields." This reminded the farmers of the importance of scattering the seed across the entire field, knowing this would lead to more plants and a greater harvest. Another adage became, "The soil is worth the toil." Many farmers—laboring hard as they worked the ground—found solace in that phrase, knowing healthy soil leads to healthy plants. It reminded them that their efforts were not in vain.

As the farmers began to see the benefits of returning to their older ways, they modified other practices too. For *example, the annual ornamental plant challenge was canceled, and in its place came the produce competition, which compared the biggest and best examples from the harvest. Adjustments like this further strengthened the mission to scatter seed and bring in a full harvest.*

And the harvest yields were increasing! This brought economic growth and expansion to the farm, but the extra produce also brought the needs of the community into focus. Many people in the countryside around the farm had little food to eat. Others ate unhealthily, eating highly processed food that provided little nutritional value. The farmers could have used their surplus to feed these people, but sadly, they never saw that opportunity.

One night while the farmers were discussing where to build new, bigger barns to hold all the extra produce, the thought dawned on them. Before they voted, one of the farmhands burst into the meeting and exclaimed, "Our produce shed has been broken into!" After some alarm— and after a few farmers suggested this is why they must build better barns—the group thought of the idea to feed the community rather than hoard their surplus.

"Farmer's Market" stands popped up everywhere, allowing people to visit conveniently for delicious produce. Then some farmers contacted a local school and inquired about providing fresh vegetables for school lunches. This created a partnership where students took field trips to the farm and farmers traveled to the school to teach about farming. The community's appreciation for the farm deepened considerably.

The farmers also developed a desire to serve their community and other communities without farms. A few moved across town to start a new farm for the express purpose of positioning fresh produce closer to consumers, while others set up community gardens to allow people to tend their own plots. A miracle was happening: not only was the farm's reputation growing, but more people were also learning to scatter seed and enjoy the nourishment from what they grew!

Principle #9: The mission is reinforced when it becomes the object of communication and celebration.

Reinforce the Goal

A church that effectively carries out its mission will do more than simply follow a set of practices that corresponds to a mission statement. The people will become passionate, even joyful, about the mission. Aubrey Malphurs writes, "Passionate people begin to live and breathe the mission. Passion is the decided difference between ministry mediocrity and ministry excellence."[57] Armed with a sense of direction, a church will also develop language and customs that reflect the mission it is pursuing. Churches reveal their true identity not in mission statements but in the everyday ways people interact and demonstrate what they value. As the Apostle John reminds us, "Little children, let us not love in word or talk but in deed and in truth" (1 John 3:18). John's point is not, of course, that loving words do not matter. But while words matter, actions demonstrate whether a church is on mission or not.

Communicate in Mission Terms

The character of any organization will be formed by the language it uses. The author of Proverbs declares, "A word fitly spoken is like apples of gold in a setting of silver" (Prov. 25:11). Words are a gift that have the power to uplift, to sharpen, to motivate. But words can also be used to tear down. Have you ever found yourself serving within a disagreeable environment with grumbling people? Eventually, their negativity sticks to you and sours your experience. Harness positive speech that builds mission momentum. Mission-positive words help spur people on as they serve. Colin Marshall and Tony Payne explain, "You want [your church's vision] to become a constant note—like the sound of a tuning fork—that resonates through your congregational life."[58] Consider how your church can spur one another toward the mission through words.

Affirmation. Words can be used powerfully to affirm people who are laboring on mission. Paul writes about people who are fearful among the believers at Thessalonica, telling them to "encourage the fainthearted" (1 Thess. 5:14). People need encouraging, affirming words to remind them that not only does their heavenly Father notice their efforts but their brothers and sisters in Christ appreciate them too. Look for ways to encourage people who are serving and helping the church in its mission. In the business world, companies understand that it is much easier to keep an existing customer than it is to gain a new one. In a similar sense, churches can help affirm existing volunteers toward mission success simply through encouraging words.

Motivation. Some people may need a little assistance mobilizing toward the mission. In many cases, they are idle simply because they cannot see where they can serve in meaning-ful ways. Creating a clear picture that helps them understand what they can do is beneficial. But others, according to Scrip-ture, are simply idle. Their ministry is nil, not because they are intimidated but because they do not value contribution toward the mission, especially their own. Still others harbor inconsequential cares that choke out their love for pursuing God's plan; for these people, Paul commands us to "admon-ish the idle" (1 Thess. 5:14). Lovingly rouse them from their spiritual stupor by reminding them that God made everyone in the Body of Christ to serve.

Calibration. The Apostle Peter used mission terms to revive the Jewish Christians who had been scattered through per-secution. They were inactive due to the troubles they had experienced for following Christ. Peter implored, "There-fore, preparing your minds for action, and being sober-minded, set your hope fully on the grace that will be brought to you at the revelation of Jesus Christ" (1 Pet. 1:13). The believers then indicated improved readiness to continue the mission. Hope for the future can calibrate the mind toward Christ's call in the present. Nerves are steeled and hearts are tuned to beat to the mission's frequency. The goal of cali-bration is to coax the inactive to be active, not to tear down anyone. Paul explains, "Let no corrupting talk come out of your mouths, but only such as is good for building up, as fits the occasion, that it may give grace to those who hear" (Eph. 4:29). Calibrate others in a way that encourages them toward greater commitment.

Supplication. Believers should pray in mission terms. The ultimate mission is the increased glory of God. Pray for

God to be glorified through your church, your volunteers, your ministry opportunities, and all related efforts. Lift up the mission to God, asking Him to bless and direct it for His purpose and glory. Paul tells the Thessalonian believers, "Rejoice always, pray without ceasing, give thanks in all circumstances; for this is the will of God in Christ Jesus for you" (1 Thess. 5:16–18). A mission without prayer is simply a set of goals to be accomplished in your own strength. Frequently lift your mission up to God and encourage your members to do the same.

When people begin praying about the mission, they open their hearts to be molded by God for His mission purposes. If prayer is treated as an add-on, God's power is perceived as optional. Without prayer, the mission becomes something we think we can accomplish in our own strength. What we pursue without prayer calls our motivation into question. Is the mission about God or about us? Are we building God's Kingdom or Babel? Through prayer, the congregation builds unity not simply around the mission but with the God who empowers it.

Celebrate Success

In the middle half of the twentieth century, Sunday school attendance pins became commonplace in many churches. Adults who met certain attendance requirements earned pins, which they displayed prominently, much like a decorated soldier. While many may dismiss this outdated form of recognition, the goal behind it was both positive and strategic. Because leaders understood that adults grow in their faith through consistent engagement in Bible study, they celebrated faithful attendance so that others may be encouraged to attend more and grow in their faith, too.

The encouragement of the pins also facilitated discipleship. Centering discipleship around the church's mission will keep associated programs vibrant and fuel the mission energy of the people. The celebration of engagement in the discipleship program helped mobilize people to carry out the mission. It was a symbiotic relationship. However, over time, many churches unconsciously shifted their discipleship focus to classroom time only, with less regard for the actual teaching and implementation of the Word. The pins lost their meaning and devolved into a personal status symbol, which soon seemed silly. Nonetheless, whether recognition comes through pins or some other avenue, it is important to celebrate personal growth through tangible encouragement.

Leaders reinforce the mission by what they celebrate. When a new small group Bible study begins, celebrate it! Share how many people the new endeavor is reaching, mark new connections made between small groups and ministry opportunities, and explain how these groups are already living out the mission of the church. On the other end of the spectrum, celebrate people who have served a long time, explaining how their service has tracked closely to the church's mission. Every celebration is, in fact, an opportunity to point people to the God who is guiding the church to carry out its disciple-making mission.

Celebration indicates God's power is alive and working. People need reminders that God is at work in their midst. God-honoring celebration signals that, by God's strength, you are accomplishing the church's mission. Without such celebration, people are robbed of the reassurance that results from seeing their efforts bear fruit. In a sense, celebration is like that mark on the doorframe where a child's height is recorded to track growth. Growth is not noticeable from a daily perspective, but a quick mark every now and then shows that progress is being made. Inspire your people by highlighting progress.

God commanded Old Testament Israel to observe various holidays and feasts, including the Passover and Feast of Tabernacles. These were not simply religious observances; they were celebrations. The people recalled their shared history and the God who had led them through it; their celebrations knit them together as the people of God.

Celebration joins the activities of the church to its mission. People may value a ministry or program, but they could use reminders about the program's purpose. If the goal of a recreational ministry is to draw new families into worship, celebrate the number of families that did so in the past year. Remind people of the goal they seek, even as they see it being accomplished. People will visually connect an activity with its intended mission outcome when they see that outcome celebrated.

What else should you celebrate? Consider this question as a leadership team. It may be a new endeavor or the conclusion of a ministry effort. Simply telling a small story about the success of a worthy activity can be a powerful means to build mission cohesion. Shining the spotlight on church members who are helping to fulfill the church's mission can encourage others to deepen their involvement. People see how those in their midst carry out the mission, and they begin to envision the ways they can contribute. Find ways to celebrate what is happening in the life of your church and watch how it helps morale flourish.

When celebrating a big accomplishment, look for ways to highlight smaller accomplishments, too. If you decide to honor the teacher who has taught for forty-five years, take a moment to call attention to your newest recruit as well. Then give glory to God for all the teachers. These small additions to the celebration will not subtract from the seasoned honoree, and they may provide potential future teachers with a better sense that they could similarly excel to God's glory over time.

How should you celebrate? There is no end to the variety of ways. Take a moment during congregational worship to celebrate—doing so during a worship service may keep the focus on praising God for His empowering work. If your church has a newsletter, include a write-up about something key to making disciples. When meeting with leaders, celebrate the work of your team, highlighting that their work is making a difference. Within each gathering, large or small, consider what you can thank God for and celebrate together.

Mobilize for Further Missions

Mission motivation should generate additional mission-related efforts. Your church has an existing set of ministries employed to carry out the mission and a certain number of people committed to serving those ministries. These are meant to reach even more people, who would in turn be mobilized for the mission. Built into the idea of the mission is a measure of expansion and change over time. As we have discussed, communication in mission terms prevents mission drift, but it also aligns people with the call to make disciples who make disciples.

Just as Jesus, the Great Commissioner, spent considerable time healing and meeting needs among the people, the church's mission efforts will naturally expand by meeting needs within the community. People who are touched by the mission will consider new ways to live it out. This burst of creative energy comes from the stability of clearly articulated mission goals. Mission communication now empowers mission mobilization later.

Advertisers understand a concept called "effective frequency," which relates to the number of ad impressions a person requires before committing. It takes from seven to twenty impressions before a person commits to a specific brand.[59] (This figure does not always relate to an actual purchase but rather to esteeming that brand as the top choice for a future purchase). People may require similar exposure to a church's mission. Christians are not selling a product, but we do seek to make an impression whenever we communicate the gospel's call. Advertising practices suggest we must be vigilant to connect the mission of the church to the actions of our members.

Patiently lay a framework of communication and allow God to build on it through the creative energies of the people He has brought into your congregational flock. Though the process takes time, stay faithful as you emphasize the church's disciple-making mission. One day, the Lord will inspect the fruit of your church. He once approached a fig tree, expecting figs. Unfortunately, none could be found. The tree looked attractive from a distance, displaying a fine trunk and leafy green foliage, but no fruit.[60] Learn from Christ's object lesson. Continue to motivate your people through the mission of the church toward fruitful disciple-making. That is, mobilize them for Christ.

Questions to Consider

1. How can a church's mission become a rallying point for the church?

2. Describe how communication in mission terms can strengthen and unify your church around the mission.

3. What does your church celebrate? How can celebration reinforce and further the mission?

4. What measurable goals could your church celebrate related to its mission? How can you most effectively celebrate them?

5. Where does your church want to go next?

EPILOGUE

One day, a man walked along the road and stopped to look at the farm. He stood on the hillside to look down at all the farming activity. He saw new crops grow-ing — young, healthy, and full of promise. He spotted a farmer harvesting some mature plants in a neighboring field. Others were seen carting fertilizer to spread on the ground. In the distance, the traveler noticed people planting in a new field. They appeared to be teenagers learning the trade from a more experienced farmer. In a berry patch there were even younger children picking the sweet, fruity treats and placing them in buckets. Not all the berries made it into the pails; several were immedi-ately popped into the children's mouths, now ringed in purplish-red hues from the juices. A few farmers could be seen loading up a truck with fresh produce ready to be shared with the community.

And the produce! There was a great deal of produce. Thirty, sixty, and even a hundred times what was sown had been reaped. That harvest did not come from every field: a few fields lay fallow, a sign that the farmers understood the land needed occasional rest. The farm-ers themselves looked as though they were well rested, appearing energized and happy. With an inclined ear, the man heard joyous shouts, whistling, and calls back and forth. Some were calls of encouragement, while others were the sort of fun jabs that come from people who care deeply for one another.

The man thought about walking further to the farm — about greeting each farmer and each guest on the farm. He considered putting his hands in the dirt to feel its earthy goodness, running his fingers along the plant leaves to enjoy their texture and life within. But instead, the man smiled and gazed upon all the activities of the farm, knowing the hurdles they had overcome and the diligence that was required to labor so faithfully.

Through a smile, he whispered, "Well done. Your Master Gardener is pleased."

ACKNOWLEDGMENTS

I am grateful for the wide variety of help and support that went into this project. At many points, encouraging responses gave me just what I needed to continue my research and writing. With that in mind, too many people provided help than I can acknowledge here, but I do not want to let that stop me from listing some whose help comes to mind.

Michael, Jessica, and the rest of the Good Comma Editing team were an invaluable help editing and proofing this work with a theological eye for detail. Likewise, Andy, Lauren, and the team at Ballast Books were a big help both in publication and with marketing.

On the more personal side, my wife and kids were incredibly patient when I needed to focus on writing. By God's grace, we navigated all the aspects of daily family life without feeling robbed of the time it took me for the project. Redland Baptist Church, where I serve, graciously gave me a sabbatical in 2019, which is when this idea and its initial writing began in Williamsburg, Virginia, with some time-share points gifted to me by Rob and Cheryl Burba.

Were it not for Maina Mwaura bringing some other writing projects my way, I likely never would have developed the resolve to get back to writing what God laid on my heart. The encouragement of other friends, family, and investors helped me stick to a plan to make this project a success.

May God use it for His glory!

APPENDICES

A CASE STUDY:
OIL CHANGE MINISTRY

*S*ome programs in the church may obscure or obstruct the disciple-making mission. They are not necessarily bad programs, but they may be off by a degree or two. Sometimes the problem is that church leaders never aligned the program with the church's mission.

Recently, Bob's pastor preached about being the hands and feet of Christ. The sermon prompted Bob to go to his pastor with an idea. What if the men in the church provided free oil changes for the single women in the community? What a great idea! The pastor asked questions about when and how often the service would be offered, when it would start, who would pay for the oil, and so on. Then he gave hearty approval for quarterly oil change events to be performed in the rear parking lot.

The program allowed the church to show love to single moms, widows, and other women in need, and thus reflected the heart of Christ through that local church.

But in retrospect, there was a problem. Despite the blessings, the oil change ministry obscured the church's mission.

1. Can you spot any potential problems with this ministry idea?

2. How could such a good ministry idea conflict with the church's mission?

Analysis

Bob's new ministry yielded at least three results. First, these women received positive and meaningful support. Second, men in the church served others in a consequential way. Third, this new ministry, lacking a well-thought-out plan, sparked confusion: was it outreach, facilitating discipleship, or simply exhibiting kindness?

In this scenario, the pastor could have provided better leadership. The pastor will stand before God as the shepherd of a church whose job is to make disciples. Bob brought him an excellent idea, which he approved without helping Bob see a significant flaw. The pastor could have asked Bob, "How does this act of kindness tie directly to the church's call to disciple people?" The ministry is not the issue; the guidance (or lack of it) toward making disciples is the issue. Answering that question would have been more difficult than determining who pays for the oil, and more importantly, a clear answer would help keep the church on mission.

The pastor could have helped Bob's promising new ministry start and stay on mission by responding, "Bob, this sounds like a great outreach. Let's talk about how we can use it to help these single women come to faith in Christ and grow in the local church. Perhaps Jan, the leader of the women's ministry, could coordinate." The pastor could have gone further by leading Bob through a brainstorming session regarding what might come from this program. Some possible outcomes:

- Women from the church show up to build relationships with the women served by the oil change ministry. While the widow is having her oil changed, a woman from the church is sitting with her to build a relationship intentionally and share her testimony.

- Single moms could get personal tours of the children's areas during the oil changes to introduce them to other ways the church could meet their needs.

- Every woman who comes in for an oil change is personally invited to the ladies' Bible study and receives a follow-up call from a woman in the Bible study.

- A special women's event is developed to coincide with the oil changes. A modest event may be coffee, donuts, and a listening ear.

- A "y'all come" invitation morphs into prescheduled oil changes, facilitating more tactical preparation beforehand to provide improved personal contact.

- Evaluations of the oil change events include metrics for how many women took a designated follow-up step, such as attending a women's study or enjoying coffee with some women from the church.

Any outreach ministry can be analyzed in this sort of manner. By the way, the same brainstorming approach could apply to the men changing the oil. Bob could develop goals for the men who do the work. For instance, some of them may volunteer to change oil because they like working on cars, but they also need to be plugged into a Bible study for men.

A positive outcome of this case study would see the pastor working with Bob to develop mission focus and deploy training to accomplish it. The men in the planning meeting would already know that their job goes way beyond the actual oil changes. It could go something like this: after Mike signed up for the oil change ministry, Pastor Bob encouraged Fred to befriend Mike and personally invite him to join his men's Bible study group. The oil change ministry thus becomes fertile ground for the men to make disciples, too. This could even become an outreach strategy beyond disconnected men within the church to those who are outside the church.

Without this mission-centered direction, the oil change program could be a disaster. Within a couple of years, the dozen men Bob recruited may dwindle to only four who are wondering why the other guys are not showing up. The women who were blessed with free oil changes appreciate the heart of the church, and perhaps a few might attend a service or two. Many others might hear about the Easter egg hunt and bring their kids, but not for the right reasons—hey, free candy is free candy! Finally, the church may codify its miscalculation by identifying the oil change ministry as a success story despite its minimal impact toward disciple-making.

A CASE STUDY:
OUTREACH EVENTS

*T*he demographics around Faith Community Church are changing. The church was established and grew decades ago during a period of suburban expansion. Now its members travel from outside the community to attend worship services faithfully, while few from the surrounding neighborhood are involved. That community has degraded a bit recently, with crime statistics headed in the wrong direction. The church members care about the community, but they do not know how to reach the people there. For many in the neighborhood, English is not their first language.

The church members know the value of good outreach events. They have a reputation for fall harvest parties, spring egg hunts, and a well-run VBS program. But they acknowledge these events reach few from their local neighborhood. Sadly, the opposite is true: the strongest attendance demographic reflects people from other churches patronizing their events. Though the church members feel unsettled by the lack of community involvement, they are a faithful flock, so they do not want to abandon the only source of outreach fruit they are experiencing, however minimal, for something unknown. Thus, they continue to hold their events as they have done in the past, hoping things will change.

Questions to Consider

1. Why might the local neighborhood not be attending Faith Community Church's outreach events?

2. How could the members of Faith Community Church better get to know the people in the community around the church?

3. How could the needs of the community be discerned so that the church could tailor its outreach efforts to them?

4. What drastic steps could the church take to get more involved in the community?

Analysis

The members of Faith Community Church are no longer part of the community; the community does not feel a connection to the church. Years ago, the call to reach the community suffered mission drift, and the church forgot to emphasize direct rather than indirect community outreach. Now the mission is obscured by good events whose targets no longer exist nearby. Church leaders would be wise to guide the church to rediscover and embrace a specific mission.

If they discern that God is leading them to reach the neighborhood once again, there will need to be a realignment of ministry priorities. Perhaps they might be led to launch a second campus outside the community so that both campuses could leverage their relative strengths to focus more on community needs. Some members may feel led to move back into the community to develop individual relationships; if so, they should consider learning the now-prevailing language(s).

Without an understanding of its mission, Faith Community Church will slowly dwindle in membership while continuing to hold the same, unchanging events.

CHILD PROTECTION

We are home gardeners. During the first year of our vegetable garden, we were amazed by the productive squash we planted. Each day brought more straight neck, zucchini, and pattypan squash than we could ever eat on our own. We ate what we could and froze or gave away the rest. Then one day, all our squash plants looked wilted. The next day, all were dead. As new gardeners, we were perplexed and a little heartbroken. What had caused this loss? We discovered that a little squash beetle had paid a rather devastating visit to our garden. When this beetle arrives, the results are quick and devastating. Had we applied a few safeguards through regular spraying, this misfortune could have been avoided.

In chapter seven, protecting children is described as a special aspect of structural safeguards in the church. Thriving churches can be dealt devastating blows without the proper safeguards in place. Your church may already have a system in place to protect children. Such systems are fantastic to review and improve over time. If your church has not yet developed a structural safeguard for children, make this a priority to avoid catastrophic harm to children, adult volunteers, families, and your congregation.

This appendix is not a comprehensive guide but rather an encouragement to get started. The key tasks to protect children include developing a child protection policy, and screening and training ministry workers.

Developing a Child Protection Policy

A child protection policy is adopted by the church and must be followed for children's ministry activities. A policy like this typically contains a purpose statement, defines the processes to screen and enlist workers, explains basic rules (i.e., the requirement to have at least two adults always present), and introduces critical protocols, such as how to respond to allegations of abuse. Any policy that is adopted should align with existing laws; therefore, an attorney should review the policy.

Some churches adopt a policy that is so thorough that it becomes difficult to follow. This can create risk in the event of an allegation of abuse because it enables a prosecuting attorney to establish that a church did not follow its own policy. To draft and refine the policy, seek out a variety of inputs from people who are especially motivated to establish an approach that both protects children and is easily executed.

Screening and Training Ministry Workers

People expect that in any childcare setting, those working with children have undergone a background check. This prevents someone with a criminal record from working with children. If your church does not have this screening process, someone already convicted of child abuse could easily work in your ministry. Ensure that every worker has received a background check.

Volunteers must also be trained so that they understand the policy and can follow it. Initial training happens during the enlistment process. Ongoing training keeps the information fresh in people's minds. Training refreshers can occur when it is time to renew the background checks, which many churches do every one to two years.

Where to Find Resources

Child protection defenses can be daunting for a church that has not undertaken this process before. Take heart! With help, you can do it, and you will quickly find it worth it; even if no allegations are ever made, many positive results ensue. First, effective enforcement of your policy may be the reason no allegations are made. Second, both parents and volunteers will feel more confident in your children's ministry, knowing the priority you place on keeping their children safe. Third, every volunteer can receive training on spotting abuse, which often happens outside the ministry setting. More children can be protected by caring adults who are vigilant for signs of abuse, whether these children are involved in your church's ministry or not.

Where can you find resources to get started? Fortunately, there are many. Here are some ideas:

- Your church's denomination may have resources in place.
- Your insurance carrier may offer policy templates or have a background check partner.
- Many ministry background check companies offer training resources to couple background checks with requisite training seamlessly.

Some organizations are well known and offer online resources. Consider these:[61]

- Protect My Ministry (https://www.protectmyministry. com/) offers both background checks and training.
- MinistrySafe (https://ministrysafe.com/) offers both background checks and training.

- Brotherhood Mutual (https://www.brotherhoodmutual.com/) offers several safety resources, including some on child safety, background checking, and guidelines for ministry workers.

- GuideOne Insurance (https://www.guideone.com/) offers several safety resources, including sample child protection policies.

- Ministry Grid (https://ministrygrid.lifeway.com/) provides free abuse prevention and response training.

ENDNOTES

[1] The labels *conservative* and *liberal* in this chapter have nothing to do with political alignment; they are theological designations.

[2] Greg L. Hawkins and Cally Parkinson, *Reveal: Where Are You?* (Barrington, IL: Willow Creek Association, 2007), 13.

[3] Amy Yotopoulos, "Three Reasons Why People Don't Volunteer, and What Can Be Done about It," Stanford Center on Longevity, accessed July 3, 2023, https://longevity.stanford.edu/three-reasons-why-people-dont-volunteer-and-what-can-be-done-about-it/.

[4] See Matthew 4:18–22.

[5] John R. W. Stott, *The Radical Disciple: Some Neglected Aspects of Our Calling* (Downers Grove, IL: IVP Books, 2010), 19.

[6] Mark Dever, *Discipling: How to Help Others Follow Jesus* (Wheaton, IL: Crossway, 2016), 15.

[7] Dever, *Discipling*, 17.

[8] Robby Gallaty, *Rediscovering Discipleship: Making Jesus' Final Words Our First Work* (Grand Rapids, MI: Zondervan, 2015), 82.

[9] Bill Hull, *The Disciple-Making Church: Leading a Body of Believers on the Journey of Faith*, updated ed. (Grand Rapids, MI: Baker Books, 2010), 15–16.

[10] Lifeway Research, "Churchgoers Believe in Sharing Faith, Most Never Do," Churchgoer Views and Practice, August 13, 2012, https://research.lifeway.com/2012/08/13/churchgoers-believe-in-sharing-faith-most-never-do/.

[11] Barna, *Reviving Evangelism: Current Realities That Demand a New Vision for Sharing Faith* (2019).

[12] Barna, "Almost Half of Practicing Christian Millennials Say Evangelism Is Wrong," Generations, February 5, 2019, https://www.barna.com/research/millennials-oppose-evangelism/.

[13] Barna, *Reviving Evangelism*.

[14] Marissa Postell Sullivan, "Research Reveals Importance of Small Groups, Evangelism, Assimilation for Church Growth," Pastor Views, Lifeway Research, March 7, 2023, https://research.lifeway.com/2023/03/07/research-reveals-importance-of-small-groups-evangelism-assimilation-for-church-growth/.

[15] Barna, "New Research on the State of Discipleship," Leadership, December 1, 2015. https://www.barna.com/research/new-research-on-the-state-of-discipleship/.

[16] See John 3:8 for an example when Jesus likens the work of the Holy Spirit to unpredictable wind.

[17] See Acts 17:6.

[18] Francis Chan, *Letters to the Church* (Colorado Springs: David C. Cook, 2018), 92.

[19] Eric Geiger and Kevin Peck, *Designed to Lead: The Church and Leadership Development* (Nashville: B&H Publishing Group, 2016), 52.

[20] John Piper, "The Marks of a Spiritual Leader," desiringGod, January 1, 1995, https://www.desiringgod.org/articles/the-marks-of-a-spiritual-leader.

[21] Robby Gallaty, *Rediscovering Discipleship: Making Jesus' Final Words Our First Work* (Grand Rapids, MI: Zondervan, 2015), 78.

[22] See Exodus 24:4–5.

[23] See James 4:13–17.

[24] See Matthew 7:21–23.

[25] Eric Guttag, "The Legacy of George Washington Carver, Tuskegee Educator, Innovator and Renaissance Man," IPWatchdog, February 12, 2014, https://ipwatchdog.com/2014/02/12/the-legacy-of-george-washington-carver-tuskegee-educator-innovator-and-renaissance-man/id=47963/.

[26] Guttag, "The Legacy of George Washington Carver."

[27] Cardinal Mazarin. In Ratcliffe, S. (Ed.), *Oxford Essential Quotations*. : Oxford University Press. Retrieved 17 Feb. 2024, https://www.oxfordreference.com/view/10.1093/acref/9780191826719.001.0001/q-oro-ed4-00016838.

[28] John Unseem, "Notes on the Sociological Study of Language," Items, March 5, 2019, https://items.ssrc.org/from-our-archives/notes-on-the-sociological-study-of-language/.

[29] See Matthew 25:14–30, where three servants receive five, two, and one talent, respectively, and Luke 19:11–27, where ten servants each receive one mina. A talent represented a large sum of money; sixty minas equaled one talent.

[30] The Greek term here for slothful, *okneros* (ὀκνηρός), shares the same root as in Matthew 25:26. That word occurs just three times in the New Testament.

[31] See 1 Peter 5:1–4.

[32] See 2 Timothy 4:2–5.

[33] Colin Marshall and Tony Payne, *The Vine Project: Shaping Your Ministry Culture around Disciple-Making* (Youngstown, OH: Matthias Media, 2016), 176.

[34] Colin Marshall and Tony Payne, *The Trellis and the Vine: The Ministry Mind-Shift That Changes Everything* (Youngstown, OH: Matthias Media, 2021), 9–10. *The Vine Project*, a sequel to this work, was quoted earlier.

[35] Robby Gallaty is the senior pastor of Long Hollow Baptist Church in Hendersonville, TN.

[36] W. Edwards Deming, *Out of the Crisis* (Cambridge, MA: MIT Press, 1982), 119.

[37] See also Colossians 2:8, 1 Timothy 6:20–21, and Jude 3.

[38] See the appendix for ideas to implement sensible child protection in your church or ministry.

[39] Aubrey Malphurs, *Advanced Strategic Planning: A New Model for Church and Ministry Leaders*, 2nd ed. (Grand Rapids, MI: Baker Books, 2005), 296.

40 Malphurs, *Advanced Strategic Planning*, 97.

41 Thom S. Rainer and Eric Geiger, *Simple Church: Returning to God's Process for Making Disciples* (Nashville: B&H Publishing Group, 2006), 48.

42 See Matthew 8:20.

43 Tony Schwartz, "Relax! You'll Be More Productive," *The New York Times*, February 9, 2013, https://www.nytimes.com/2013/02/10/opinion/sunday/relax-youll-be-more-productive.html.

44 Eric Geiger and Kevin Peck, *Designed to Lead: The Church and Leadership Development* (Nashville: B & H Publishing Group, 2016), 87.

45 Kennon L. Callahan, *Effective Church Finances: Fund-Raising and Budgeting for Church Leaders* (San Francisco: Jossey-Bass Publishers, 1997), 3.

46 See Matthew 25:21.

47 Aubrey Malphurs, *Advanced Strategic Planning: A New Model for Church and Ministry Leaders*, 2nd ed. (Grand Rapids, MI: Baker Books, 2005), 266.

48 Geiger and Peck, *Designed to Lead*, 154.

49 Alvin J. Lindgren, *Foundations for Purposeful Church Administration* (New York: Abingdon Press, 1965), 69.

50 See Acts 2:40–47.

51 See 2 Kings 4:4–7.

[52] Alan Raughton, "Provide Space and Resources," Ken Braddy and Allan Taylor, comps., *Building a Disciple-Making Ministry: The Timeless Principles of Arthur Flake for Sunday School and Small Groups* (Nashville: Lifeway Press, 2020), 63.

[53] That does sound like a great mash-up event, and maybe there is something to that. See the next section on allocating creatively.

[54] Dr. Conway Edwards shared this account with me during an interview about the early days of One Community Church.

[55] See Exodus 14.

[56] See Joshua 3.

[57] Aubrey Malphurs, *Advanced Strategic Planning: A New Model for Church and Ministry Leaders*, 2nd ed. (Grand Rapids, MI: Baker Books, 2005), 140.

[58] Colin Marshall and Tony Payne, *The Vine Project: Shaping Your Ministry Culture around Disciple-Making* (Youngstown, OH: Matthias Media, 2016), 309.

[59] "Say It Again: Messages Are More Effective When Repeated," The Financial Brand, September 23, 2014, https://thefinancialbrand.com/news/bank-marketing/advertising-marketing-messages-effective-frequency-42323/.

[60] See Mark 11:12–14.

[61] Use your best judgment, of course, when choosing these resources. It is wise to seek legal counsel and other ministry expertise.

Milton Keynes UK
Ingram Content Group UK Ltd.
UKHW011134220424
441551UK00006B/530

9 781962 202633